BULBS
FOR ALL SEASONS

· GARDENING · BY · DESIGN ·

BULBS
FOR ALL SEASONS

· PHILIP · SWINDELLS ·

Ward Lock Limited · London

© Ward Lock Ltd 1987

First published in Great Britain in 1987
by Ward Lock Limited, 8 Clifford Street
London W1X 1RB, an Egmont Company.

House editor Denis Ingram
Text set in Bembo
by TJB Photosetting Ltd, South Witham, Lincolnshire

Printed and bound in France by
Brodard

British Library Cataloguing in Publication Data

Swindells, Philip
  Bulbs for all seasons.—— (Gardening by
  design)
  1. Bulbs   2. Flowers
  I. Title   II. Series
  ISBN 0-7063-6529-1

CONTENTS

PREFACE 6

1 A CAVALCADE OF SPRING COLOUR 7

2 BULBS OF HIGH SUMMER 21

3 AUTUMN AND WINTER COLOUR 33

4 USING BULBS IN BEDS AND BORDERS 41

5 BRIGHTENING WINDOW BOXES AND PLANTERS 48

6 BULBS IN POTS AND BOWLS 53

7 BULB PROBLEMS 68

APPENDICES: 1 Selecting and buying bulbs 73
2 Propagating bulbs and corms 75
3 Cut flower bulbs 76
4 Classification 77

INDEX 79

PREFACE

Bulbs are the most attractive and versatile of flowering plants, and whether you have extensive beds and borders, a terrace or patio, or just a pot on the window ledge, there is a bulb for you. From the enormous and brightly coloured trumpets of the amaryllis to the delicate nodding blossoms of miniature daffodils there is something for everyone. Bulbs can be used in bold masses, for adding highlights to the garden, scattering in a grassy sward or regimenting in a bowl at Christmas time. The opportunities for using them are legion, and yet they are amongst the easiest plants to grow. And most important of all, almost every purchase guarantees a flower, because when you buy a bulb the bud is already formed inside. All you do is plant it and wait.

Hopefully this book will encourage the wider use of bulbs in the home and garden. Not only those that are truly bulbs, but corms and tubers as well.

P.S.

ACKNOWLEDGEMENTS

The publishers are grateful to the following persons and agencies for granting permission for the following colour photographs to be reproduced: Michael Warren (pp. 10, 11, 14, 50, 63 & 66); Enid Pyrah (p. 27); Harry Smith Horticultural Photographic Collection (p. 30); Dutch Bulb Council (p.31); Michael Boys (pp.3, 34, 35, 43, 51, & 70); Tania Midgeley (pp. 39, 42, 54, 55, 58 & 71); and Bob Challinor (p. 62). The photographs on pp. 15, 19, 22, 23, 59 & 74 were taken by Bob Challinor.

All the line drawings were drawn by Pamela Dowson.

1

A CAVALCADE OF SPRING COLOUR

While most gardeners are happy with a spring bulb display arranged in a somewhat formal manner, the more adventurous choose to integrate their bulbs in the overall garden plan. Some bulbs like hyacinths and tulips must have a formal setting if they are to look their best as they are very formal plants, but all the rest can be mixed happily with other subjects to create spring highlights in the garden.

Ornamental shrubs give the gardener the greatest opportunity for painting a colourful spring picture with bulbs. Plant the low-growing grape hyacinth, *Muscari* 'Blue Spike', beneath yellow forsythia and associate the lovely creamy-white *Narcissus cyclamineus* 'Jenny' with the carmine flowered *Ribes sanguineum*, the flowering currant. Dwarf anemones like the blue-flowered *Anemone blanda* and its colourful named varieties can be scattered amongst any shrubby planting. They naturalize freely and open bright daisy-like blossoms to the sun. Foxtail lilies or eremurus are the kings of the late spring and early summer garden, with towering spires of blossom in pink, yellow and white. Plant them behind low-growing shrubs so that their fading leaves can be disguised. Do the same with crown imperials, *Fritillaria imperialis*. These are the lovely bulbous plants favoured by Dutch painters with bright orange or yellow pendant bell-like blossoms and terminal tufts of bright green foliage.

Carpet the front of a shrub border with squills. These are cheap and cheerful bulbs that spread freely and need little attention. A sea of the dark blue *Scilla sibirica* to set afloat towering conifers, or a rivulet of pale blue *S. tubergeniana* to highlight a shady bank. Plant snowdrops amongst evergreen ground cover like

ivy and periwinkle so that their pristine blossoms twinkle in the grey winter light. Introduce winter aconites to gloomy corners that are heavily shaded by trees. These will turn up their golden blossoms to an open sky long before the leaf canopy closes in.

Do not neglect bulbs as complimentary plants to herbaceous perennials. The more unusual kinds like alliums or ornamental onions integrate quite freely. Plant them in bold groups and they will behave in most respects like ordinary border plants. Be adventurous with bulb planting. Most of the popular kinds associate happily with other plants both visually and culturally.

SPRING HIGHLIGHTS

Spring flowering bulbs (Fig.1) provide even the inexperienced gardener with an opportunity to produce first class flowers. When planting a bulb, providing that you follow a few simple common sense rules, you are almost guaranteed blossoms. The buds of next spring's flowers are already formed amongst the leaf scales of each bulb when you buy it. Always purchase the most expensive bulbs that you can afford. Because they are more substantial, and provided they are sound and healthy, you will obtain much better results than from a cheap mixture. It is fair to say that there is no such thing as a good cheap bulb.

Deciding what to grow is more difficult nowadays, for not only is there diversity, but similarity. Many narcissus varieties and those of a number of tulips are

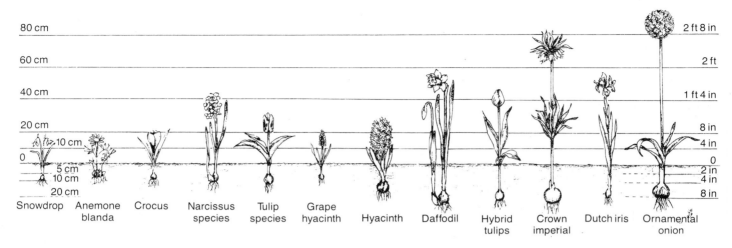

Fig. 1 Popular spring-flowering bulbs – autumn planting.

inseparable to the home gardener, but may well have specific characteristics which are not readily apparent. With daffodils of similar appearance, for example, you may well discover that one is ideal for forcing indoors, while another is better for outdoor planting. So make a careful study of the bulb growers' catalogues at the outset. Cultivars of similar appearance often have widely differing flowering periods and this should be taken into consideration when deciding what to grow.

Daffodils

Daffodils and tulips are obviously the most popular spring flowering bulbs, both being available in a diversity of shape, size, colour and form that offers something for everyone. Daffodils are botanically *Narcissus*, although to gardeners daffodils are those which have large trumpets, while narcissus are the small-cupped varieties. Newcomers to gardening will probably be tempted to select old well tried kinds like 'Carlton', 'Golden Harvest' and 'King Alfred'. Dependable though these may be, they have nowadays been surpassed by modern free-flowering sorts such as

'Spellbinder', 'Rembrandt' and the appropriately named 'Unsurpassable'. All are a rich golden yellow, except for 'Spellbinder' which is an irridescent sulphurous shade. Not all daffodils are yellow though, 'Ice Follies' being a cool icy-white, while 'Mrs.R.O. Backhouse' is shell-pink. Some are fully double, like the aged but invaluable 'Texas' and equally endearing 'Inglescombe'. The small-cupped kinds that gardeners loosely refer to as narcissus are typified by 'Geranium' and 'Actaea'. Both have broad flat white petals and orange or red cups.

Tulips

Tulips offer us equal diversity, with some varieties flowering in early spring and others in late spring. Like narcissus, tulips fall into clearly defined groups, which although having no botanical significance, are widely accepted by gardeners to identify different kinds. Single early tulips are short-growing kinds, typified by 'Kreizerskroon', the red and gold tulip of public conservatories. While many of the recent introductions within this group can be used for pot culture, they grow just as well outdoors. Flowering during mid-spring, they are more commonly used in formal planting schemes, although there is no reason why they should not provide colourful spring highlights in the informal garden. Darwin tulips are late flowering and are popularly used for spring bedding with a carpet of forget-me-nots. 'Rose Copeland' has lovely blossoms of carmine and silvery rose, while 'Princess Elizabeth' is pink and 'William Pitt' vivid scarlet. It is from the union of these two groups that the Triumph tulips have been derived. Similar in many ways to Darwins, they flower much earlier and are of shorter habit.

Most tulips are more useful in the formal garden and are discussed in Chapter 4. The species tulips and their hybrids are very popular and make excellent subjects for informal gardens, especially those that are exposed and windy. Not only are they tough and resilient, but of a much neater habit. They are a diversity of characters which can be accommodated in a wide range of situations provided they are in full sun. In recent years work with *Tulipa fosteriana*, *T. eichleri*, *T. kaufmanniana* and *T. greigii* has yielded a wealth of hybrids, all neat and colourful and compact, and well suited to the smaller modern garden. This quartet of plants are amongst the most colourful in the spring garden, the immense and startling scarlet blossoms of *T. fosteriana* presenting an unforgettable spectacle. The waterlily tulip, *T. kaufmanniana* is much shorter and of variable colour, although the habit of each variation is uniform. The common kind is believed to be creamy-white with a golden centre and a pinkish flush to the buds; it is typified by a long slender, somewhat incongrous bud nestling amongst broad glaucous foliage.

Tulipa greigii is a little gem from Central Asia with scarlet, or very occasionally rich golden yellow blossoms on much taller stout erect stems. It is a welcome harbinger of spring and one of the most robust and useful species for general garden work. *Tulipa eichleri* is equally valuable, but requires a free-draining soil in a warm situation if it is to prosper. Flowering from mid-spring onwards, it has expansive scarlet blossoms above broad glaucous foliage that is tinged and edged with maroon. *Tulipa praestans* and its cultivar 'Fusilier'

are magnificent spring-flowering bulbs with attractive green foliage and fine upstanding flower spikes, each bearing three or four blossoms and creating a startling effect when planted boldly in groups. Sadly few gardeners take advantage of these multi-headed delights, having formed the opinion that large-flowered tulips should be borne on a single stem, even if they cannot match the vermilion-scarlet of *T. praestans* and its progeny.

Smaller multi-flowered species like *T. tarda* seem to be more readily accepted and command wide appreciation, producing four or five sparkling white and gold blossoms on each stem. *Tulipa tarda* is later flowering than most, but this is no hindrance. One of the first to flower is the lovely lilac-pink and yellow *T. saxatilis*. Of modest proportions, this delicate beauty first opens its satiny blossoms during early spring. Biologically this display is futile as fertile seed is never set; instead the plant increases from creeping stolons.

Chionodoxa

Apart from tulips and narcissus there are a host of other equally worthwhile bulbs, including *Chionodoxa luciliae*, the glory of the snow, a vigorous species which seeds freely and rapidly forms an expansive carpet. It can compete with all but the most pernicious weeds and is ideal for planting amongst shrubs and roses where its starry white and blue blossoms present a spring picture that is difficult to equal. The famous botanist George Maw, on first encountering *Chionodoxa luciliae* in the wild, is quoted as having exclaimed '… One of the most sumptuous displays of floral beauty I have ever beheld', sentiments with which the majority of gardeners wholeheartedly agree.

Muscari

Grape hyacinths run chionodoxa a close second when it comes to selecting bulbs for underplanting shrubs. While the common *Muscari armeniacum* is recom-

Daffodils naturalized in a grass sward present a picture of magical beauty every spring. The stark silvery trunks of the birch frame the scene.

Snowdrops naturalized amongst hazel bushes in a wild corner of the garden.

mended for general garden use, the pale blue *M. botryoides* can look breathtaking when spread beneath the heavily laden golden boughs of *Forsythia* 'Lynwood Gold'.

Fritillaria

Another useful spring-flowering bulb is our native snakeshead lily or guinea flower, *Fritillaria meleagris*. With its delicate chequered blossoms in shades of purple, pink or cream, and slender grassy foliage of a soft glaucous hue, it is one of the most welcome flowers of spring. Its natural home is damp pastures and woodland fringes where if left to its own devices it forms spreading colonies. The tiny bulbs appear to be scaleless, but in fact consist of two or three fleshy scales, which if exposed to the air for any length of time shrivel up and die. Care must be taken when handling any fritillaria bulbs as they are easily damaged and quickly succumb to storage moulds. Always plant as early in the autumn as possible to prevent desiccation. *Fritillaria meleagris* is a very variable species, and although there are some good strong colours around, a mixture will often yield a number of washed-out shades. Where small groups are being planted, then it is preferable to depend upon the uniformity of some of the cultivars. 'Charon' is rich deep purple, 'Aphrodite' white, while 'Artemis' is greyish-purple with pronounced chequering and 'Poseidon' sports large blossoms of soft rosy purple.

Of the other fritillaries the crown imperial, *F. imperialis* is the most impressive. Beloved of Dutch painters and English cottage gardeners, this is a bold early flowering plant with glossy fresh green leaves and stout stems up to a metre high. These support clusters of large red, orange or yellow pendant bells. There are many forms of *F. imperialis*, but the most usual have orange or orange-red flowers. The variety *lutea* and *lutea maxima* have bright yellow blossoms. Those of 'Aurora' are deep jaffa-orange, *rubra maxima* red, and 'Orange Brilliant' a rich rusty hue. Crown imperials enjoy a moist soil in an open situation protected from the prevailing wind. As they possess a curious odour, they are best viewed from afar – certainly never consider them for a border near the house.

Fritillaria persica is another substantial species. Often growing to a height of 75 cm (2½ ft), it has strong stems with a bluish-grey bloom and loose racemes of deep purple bell-shaped flowers with a misty sheen. The first blossoms are produced during early spring, often a full month before the equally gardenworthy *F. pyreniaca*. Although smaller in stature, this is easier going, spreading freely in a situation to its liking. A native of short cropped grass of the Pyrenean mountain slopes, it has substantial deep purplish-brown bells on slender arching stems. It is a variable species, but one which is ideal for naturalizing where it can remain undisturbed.

Anyone who has known the fritillaries cannot fail to have been enchanted by *F. camschatcensis*, even though the botanists have recently changed its name and it is no longer a fritillary. A modest plant, no more than 35 cm (14 in) high, this is the toast of alpine specialists, even though it does not demand alpine conditions. In fact it is not too difficult to grow in any moist position where there is dappled shade. The main attraction for most gardeners is the colour of the flower, allegedly the closest that can be obtained to a true black. In reality it is a very dark plum-purple, although there is a variety called 'Black Knight' that is darker still.

Allium

None of the ornamental onions or alliums can aspire to such fame. These are amongst the cheapest and the easiest of all spring and early summer-flowering bulbs. They can be accommodated in most soils and situations, the smell of the foliage when handled being the only clue to their affinity with their temperamental kitchen garden cousins. The dried bulbs which come to hand during the autumn look like small onions, but unlike the domestic kind they need planting in the soil rather than growing on the surface. Cover the bulbs by about their own depth of soil and plant informally at distances which will allow the bulbs room to develop.

Look out for the lovely *Allium sphaerocephalum* with its dark purple bell-shaped flowers in dense umbels on stems 40 cm (16 in) high. A European native it is quite at home in our unpredictable climate. Try the short growing *A. ostrowskianum*, an amenable plant for the smaller garden where its delicate blossoms will provide a bold splash of pink during late spring. If you really want to surprise your gardening friends, then grow the spectacular *A. giganteum*. A startling plant with stems a metre high and densely packed globular heads of deep lilac flowers. Magnificent for either the wild garden or mixed border, it is a floral artist's delight. Not only are the flowers worthy of cutting, but more especially are the seed heads. When allowed to dry naturally, these become huge skeletonized balls which are perfect for dried floral arrangements. It is unlikely that the seeding heads of the charming little yellow flowered *A. moly* would be picked and dried, for this is essentially a bulb for naturalizing. It will quickly fill a secluded corner, spreading quickly from seed and providing complete cover within a couple of seasons.

Iris

Dutch iris are a very different proposition. These handsome plants are grown primarily for cutting or else standing guard in the herbaceous border. They are slender characters with strong smooth stems and beautifully sculptured blossoms. There are many lovely varieties to choose from, but the best loved is unquestionably the light blue 'Wedgwood', a fine early flowering kind with distinctive yellow markings. 'White Superior', 'Golden Harvest' and the dark blue 'Imperator' are all worthy companions. Unlike the ordinary flag iris their glory is not fleeting, individual stems lasting for at least two weeks. However, do not regard them primarily as cut flowers for they are equally suited to garden decoration, bold groups in a border persisting for years on all but the heaviest of soils. Treat them very much like daffodils or tulips,

planting in the autumn in an open sunny situation on well drained soil. Cover the bulbs with about 5 cm (2 in) of soil and plant 6 to 8 cm (2⅜ to 3 in) apart for a good effect. As shoots appear in the spring it is a wise precaution to scatter a few slug pellets about. Unless they have been planted in an exposed position, Dutch iris will require no staking. Indeed they require little attention from planting until flowering, and afterwards should be allowed to die down naturally.

AFTERCARE OF BULBS

The key to successful bulb growing is the aftercare. Anyone can provide a spectacular spring show for one season if good healthy bulbs are selected. Repeating the feat is quite another matter. Bulbs that have been properly cared for already have next season's flowering potential within them when they become dormant. Just cut a dormant bulb lengthways and you will see the embryo buds. How numerous or productive these are likely to be in the spring almost entirely depends upon the conditions under which the bulbs were growing the previous year. Neglect after flowering is always reflected in the following season's display.

To obtain the best blossoms it is necessary to grow bulbs on land that is in good heart. Where there are long-standing plantings it is vital to feed the bulbs, either with a generous spring application of bonemeal, or a liquid feed after flowering when the leaves are still green. This latter course of action needs undertaking carefully in order to prevent rapid foliage development and the production of soft bulbs which may succumb to moulds and rots during the winter. Provided they are kept weed-free, most spring-flowering bulbs present no problems. However, it is most important for their continued success to encourage foliage development and persistence after flowering. The main function of the foliage is to develop the bulb for next year and ensure the initiation of flower buds. By the time that the leaves have died down, next spring's display is latent within the bulbs and no amount of

Narcissus cyclamineus derives its name from its cyclamen-like blossoms. It is one of the easiest miniature daffodils to establish.

Tangled informality beneath a magnolia tree where bright red tulips associate with blue muscari, while primroses wink from the sidelines.

feeding or replanting will have any effect. Unsightly bulb foliage is a constant source of irritation, but it is important that it remains as long as possible. Recent experiments have shown with narcissus that it is possible to cut the leaves after six weeks. This does not apply to all cultivars or any other kinds of bulbs, so this should be done very carefully. It is still preferable to allow the foliage to die down quite naturally. The period of time that this takes varies from one bulb to another, but most spring-flowering subjects have died back by mid-summer.

ALPINE DELIGHTS

Daffodils

Of all the dwarf bulbs, it is the miniature daffodils that are the easiest to accommodate on the rock garden. Most are miniature versions of the large flowered kinds, complete in every detail, but rarely growing more than 15 cm (6 in) high. The Tenby daffodil, *Narcissus lobularis*, is one of the best known amongst these, although *N. nanus* and *N. asturiensis* are popular. The hoop petticoat daffodils are very different, their expanded globular trumpets looking rather like delicate bells clustered amongst fine rush-like foliage. The true hoop petticoat is *N. bulbocodium*, but the improved variety *conspicuus* is the kind usually offered by bulb merchants and garden centres. Although a very popular rock garden subject, the hoop petticoat is amenable to being naturalized in grass, particularly if maintained as an alpine meadow. The same could be said for *N. cyclamineus*, that curious little daffodil which has laid back petals reminiscent of a cyclamen, and a narrow protruding trumpet. Rarely more than 15 cm (6 in) high, the bright yellow *N. cyclamineus* is far superior to any of its progeny for rock garden cultivation. The charming little *N. juncifolius* has slender leaves rather like those of a rush and multiflowered heads of fragrant bright yellow blossoms; an amiable companion for *N. cyclamineus* in the rock garden.

Tulips

Amongst the tulips there are a number of species which benefit from being grown in the well drained conditions provided by a rock garden. That is not to say that other species and their garden varieties cannot be grown successfully here, for there are few more gratifying sights than a group of *Tulipa kaufmanniana* braving bitter early-spring winds on a rocky crag. If you have a rock garden be adventurous, growing those that require such conditions and removing the more amenable species to the open garden. Create gasps of admiration for the intense crimson blossoms of *T. linifolia*, a species that will only prosper in a well drained pocket on the rock garden. Even then it is short-lived and will require periodic replacement. It is well worth persisting with, for along with *T. tarda* it is one of the late blooming kinds and extends the tulip season well into late spring. A close ally, *T. maximowiczii* looks very similar, but flowers at least two weeks earlier.

Alpine house

Dwarf bulbs need not just be confined to the rock garden. Many enthusiasts now turn their unheated greenhouse into an alpine house for the first three or four months of the year. An alpine house has no artificial heat, or if it does it is only used to dispel moisture-laden air on a damp foggy morning. It is never used for raising the temperature and promoting growth. Alpine plants and dwarf bulbs are usually grown in pans and displayed around the greenhouse on staging, although some gardeners bed the pans in a gritty medium on the staging in order to create a more natural landscaped effect. This cannot be unreservedly recommended, for the gravel used to disguise the pans often harbours woodlice and similar minor pests.

Once again the dwarf narcissus are perfect subjects to grow and easy to maintain. Try the early spring flowering *N. canaliculatus* with its fragrant bunches of white and yellow flowers on stems no more than 20 cm

(8 in) high. Not all narcissus flower in the spring, some like the rather unusual *N. elegans* make a brave effort in the autumn. This, and the smaller and not dissimilar *N. serotinus*, are not the easiest bulbs to coax into flower but are well worth seeking out and trying. So too is the remarkable dwarf green-flowered *N. viridiflorus*. Although unusual rather than beautiful, it is well worth growing, seeming to enjoy the restrictions imposed by a small pot or pan.

Myriad other dwarf bulbs, corms and tubers can find a place in the alpine house. Cyclamen, colchicum, crocus and allium all enjoy life under glass and with careful selection provide an extended flowering period. But it is the irises that are the most useful of all. *Iris histrio* and *I. histrioides*, two closely related and mischievously named species herald the arrival of the new year with a display that may last until early February. *Iris histrio* is of variable colour, from soft lilac to purple, while *I. histrioides* is a clear royal blue. The common blue *I. reticulata* follows closely behind, together with the lemon-yellow *I. danfordiae* and the lovely fragrant mauve-blue *I. bakeriana*. However, the most desirable of the dwarf reticulate kinds is the pale sulphurous-yellow *I. winogradowii*.

BULBS FOR NATURALIZING

The naturalizing of bulbs is the establishment of suitable varieties in a grassy sward (Figs. 2 & 3) which can

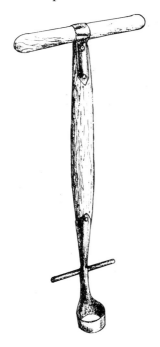

Fig. 2 A bulb planter can remove a plug of soil with little effort.

Fig. 3 Planting in grass is simplified with a bulb planter.

be left uncut after flowering until the bulb foliage has died down. The intention of this method of cultivation is to provide colour in a part of the garden which perhaps is difficult to maintain other than in grass, and to provide the most attractive background for certain selected species. Often bulbs are planted into an established sward, so it is important to choose varieties that will not only tolerate such competition, but look visually not too far removed from the original species. This applies especially to narcissus.

Narcissus

The named varieties of *Narcissus cyclamineus* are highly commended on all counts. Look out for yellow cultivars like 'February Gold' or 'Peeping Tom' as well as the creamy-white 'Jenny'. Try the multi-headed dwarf *N*. 'Tête-à-Tête' which provides delicate waving sheets of blossom which attempt to emulate our native daffodil. Closer examination reveals the plant's fraudulent nature, but the casual observer would be hard pressed to decide whether *N. lobularis* was the real thing. When choosing narcissus, think not only of trying to create an authentic effect with a cheap alternative, but give careful consideration to multi-flowered sorts as these can be planted at wider distances to give the same visual effect. Where you require a hundred bulbs of a conventional kind, you may only need seventy-five of a multi-headed cultivar to provide the same visual effect.

Galanthus

Snowdrops are also good bulbs to naturalize, especially the common single flowered *Galanthus nivalis*. Apart from giving us hope of spring to come, they flower before the grass starts growing and their foliage fades at around the time that you want to make the first cut. If the foliage is green and lively avoid cutting the grass in which they are growing until the leaves turn brown at the tips. It is essential that the leaves are

allowed to develop fully if a decent show of flowers is expected next season. While it is better to plant snowdrops in leaf, it is impractical to plant them like this in grass. Dry bulbs planted during the autumn are the easiest to deal with. Select the area in which the bulbs are to be established and then turn back the turf and cultivate the exposed soil. The bulbs should be gently scattered over this and planted where they fall if a natural effect is to be achieved. Scarcely cover the bulbs with soil as the thickness of the turf will add to the depth at which they are planted. A similar planting technique can be adopted with other naturalized bulbs.

Alpine Meadows

In the smaller garden another form of naturalizing can be adopted: the alpine meadow, a low growing sward of grass in which some small bulbous plants and alpines become established. Usually alpine meadows are colonized by hoop petticoat daffodils and an assortment of fritillarias and squills. In the average garden mixed alpines are largely ignored and the hoop petticoat daffodil and snakeshead fritillary are usually employed as the dominant species creating an alpine meadow. This is very similar to ordinary naturalizing, but can rarely be done in the usual way, that is lifting the turf and planting beneath, or planting through the grass. Apart from the difficulty of small bulb size, the grass that is used should be compatible. Long, coarse grass not only swamps the daffodils visually, but competes vigorously for nutrients and after a few years the daffodils are likely to fade away. So a suitable grass mixture has to be sown immediately after the bulbs are planted.

The best way to establish successfully an alpine meadow is to cultivate the intended area during the summer months before planting. This ensures that any coarse grass or pernicious perennial weeds are eliminated. The bulbs are usually available during early autumn and should be planted immediately. To obtain a natural look, gently scatter the bulbs over the surface of the soil and plant them where they fall. Firm the soil

Modern daffodils in a grassy setting help to lighten the heavy tone of the Lenten roses.

after planting and then sow grass seed. This need not be a special mixture, but it should comprise the finer grasses and include a greater proportion of fescues. Any weeds that appear in the seedling grass should be removed, but do not use a lawn weedkiller as this can sometimes have an effect upon emerging bulbs.

The bulbs will flower during early to mid-spring and afterwards should be allowed to die down naturally. The grass can then be cut with a rotary mower. Do not allow the grass to remain as tall as in other areas where you have naturalized bulbs, or else coarser species will start to dominate. Close cropping keeps these undesirable grasses at bay, which in turn reduces root competition with the bulbs. Feeding need not be generous, but the bulbs will appreciate a general application of bonemeal at the rate of a handful to the square metre after flowering and this will certainly not harm the grass either.

Naturalizing bulbs offers a great many opportunities for the enthusiastic gardener to experiment. Considerable research is being undertaken now by the landscape industry to see which of the popular spring- and summer-flowering bulbs will grow happily in grass. Recent work has proved that in a light or medium loam soil many of the species tulips will naturalize happily. Amongst these the most successful to date has been the lovely little *Tulipa kaufmanniana* and its cultivars, although all the shorter growing tulips are worth experimenting with. If you are a traditionalist and want to naturalize bulbs that have proved themselves over and over again, then try *Scilla non-scripta*, or as we should call it now, *Endymion campanulatus*. This is the common bluebell of the British countryside and a first class plant for naturalizing in dappled shade. The Spanish bluebell *E. hispanicus*, is a larger version and often available in named varieties. Look out especially for the deep blue 'Excelsior', although the white flowered 'Mount Everest' and lilac-pink 'Queen of the Pinks' provide an interesting variation.

2

BULBS OF HIGH SUMMER

It is usual to associate flowering bulbs with spring. Few gardeners consider them as a serious proposition for the summer garden, except perhaps for lilies. This is a shame, for there are many interesting and colourful subjects that can provide a dazzling display of colour from mid-summer until the first autumn frosts. Not only are they cheap and cheerful, but when you buy a bulb you are almost certainly guaranteed a flower, for the embryo bud is nestling within and just waiting to burst into blossom. This is not always the case with other summer flowering plants. Of course another reason why summer-flowering bulbs are not so readily considered is that they mostly come from the warmer climates of Asia, South Africa and South America. This, coupled with their exotic blossoms and general tropical aspect lead the uninitiated to believe that they must be difficult to grow. Nothing could be further from the truth, even in the colder parts of the country tigridias and eucomis can be grown successfully.

It is usual to plant summer-flowering bulbs (Fig.4) during spring, but with modern commercial storage techniques it is now possible to buy and plant over a longer period. This extends the flowering season and creates maximum impact. Lilies can, for example, be planted over a period of three months, the more recent plantings being established in front of the earlier ones. This ensures that the taller, earlier-planted bulbs flower above the foliage of more recent additions and these in turn hide the fading leaves of those that flower first. The opportunities for visual innovation are many, but for gardeners with an uncomprising clay soil there are practical merits too. So often spring-planted bulbs struggle in cold wet conditions and suffer an onslaught

from slugs. Now that bulbs can be stored for a much longer period, an opportunity can be taken to plant when conditions are just right.

The implications for flower arrangers are considerable as well, for not only does delayed planting extend the flowering period of individual bulbs, but gives a unique opportunity to plant for some unusual associations. Some flowers not usually seen together when grown under ordinary garden conditions can be fooled into blooming at the same time by carefully controlled planting. Used sensibly, delayed planting can provide many opportunities for the inventive gardener. Remember that this is a relatively new innovation and cannot be used for some of the more obscure summer-flowering bulbs, but most of the popular kinds respond, although it is only effective during the first season for those that remain in the ground over winter.

A LOOK AT LILIES

Lilies are amongst the loveliest of summer-flowering bulbs. With exotic-looking blossoms they are often regarded by the newcomer to gardening as difficult. Nothing could be further from the truth, for while there are one or two notorious kinds, the popular garden varieties that most gardeners grow are easy to satisfy. The majority prefer dappled shade and a moisture retentive soil which does not become water-logged during winter.

There are countless varieties of lilies to choose from, as any good bulb catalogue will reveal. Amongst the

Where bulbs can be naturalized around the edge of a manicured lawn aftercare is more easily and tidily achieved.

Native snakeshead fritillaries, *Fritillaria meleagris*, are happy when naturalized in a damp grassy corner.

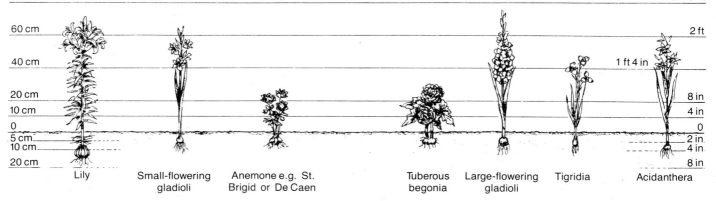

80 cm							2 ft 8 in
60 cm							2 ft
40 cm							1 ft 4 in
20 cm							8 in
10 cm							4 in
0							0
5 cm							2 in
10 cm							4 in
20 cm							8 in

Lily   Small-flowering gladioli   Anemone e.g. St. Brigid or De Caen   Tuberous begonia   Large-flowering gladioli   Tigridia   Acidanthera

Fig. 4 Popular summer-flowering bulbs – spring planting.

most reliable are the mid-century hybrids which are available in a wide range of colours and with flowers that are good for cutting as well as border decoration. They are robust characters with strong flower stems that rarely need supporting. Others are not quite as versatile, but more spectacular, the golden-rayed lily of Japan, *Lilium auratum*, and the regal lily, *L. regale*, for example. Both have magnificent trumpet-shaped blossoms in white and gold which possess a rich spicy fragrance. The lovely early summer flowering Madonna lily, *L. candidum*, has a charm all of its own, along with that other frequent resident of older gardens, the tiger lily, *L. tigrinum*. *Lilium speciosum* and its variety *rubrum* extend the flowering season into the autumn, flaunting lovely waxy blossoms of crimson and white, while the summer flowering *L. henryi* with its finely sculptured orange blossoms, and the shorter growing purple-maroon *L. martagon* are amongst the best kinds for naturalizing in grass, especially in shady parts of the garden.

Recent developments in storage methods have increased the period of time over which lilies can be planted, but most gardeners still plant during spring. The only exception is the Madonna lily, *L. candidum*, which must make a rosette of over-wintering foliage before the winter months. This must be planted during late summer. Most lilies prefer a free-draining soil of acid persuasion, and on heavier land benefit

from a generous quantity of sharp sand or grit incorporated into the soil before planting. At the very least a sprinkling of sand in the bottom of the hole for the bulb to sit on should be provided. This will enable the roots to make a better start. If your soil is not in first-class condition, then there is no reason why the bulbs cannot be potted individually in a good potting compost. They can then be transferred to their permanent positions when they have made a good rootball and the weather and outdoor soil conditions are improved.

Take care when purchasing lily bulbs. Unlike tulips and daffodils they are very fleshy and vulnerable to drying out. Only buy bulbs from a retailer who has looked after them properly. Even when being sold in the shop or garden centre they should be kept in sawdust or peat to prevent drying out. Good quality pre-packed bulbs are very good as very little air is able to get at them. However, they must be kept under cool conditions if they are not going to start sprouting. If you see any sprouted bulbs avoid them as they will not make very good plants the first year.

Lily bulbs consist largely of fleshy scales and it is from these that most of the popular varieties are propagated. At planting time scales often become detached from the parent bulb. Rather than waste them why not grow them? Provided they are not dried out and come away with a little piece of the basal plate they should grow. Of course you can deliberately break up one or two bulbs if you want to increase a particular variety in large numbers. Take the scales with a sliver of base plate and plant them in a good soil-based potting compost with about a quarter by volume of sharp sand and a similar amount of good quality sedge peat (Fig. 5). Scales inserted in trays of compost during the traditional dormant period root readily by mid-summer and often produce a few leaves. Pot the plantlets up in the same kind of compost used for starting the scales into growth and stand them in a frame. It depends upon the variety, but the scales should produce bulbs of flowering size within three to five years. Whether they spend their entire life in a frame or are planted out in the open ground after the first year is a decision each gardener has to take given his particular circumstances. Except on the heaviest land, early planting in their permanent home is most desirable.

A number of lily species are increased from seed, but this is mostly a very lengthy and time-consuming business. The best alternative is to lift and divide established clumps every five or six years. Apart from increasing your stock, it is also beneficial to the bulbs, which by that time are beginning to look a little congested. An alternative means of propagation offered by many modern hybrids and a number of species is the little purplish-brown bulbils which arise in the leaf axils. If planted in a good potting compost and afforded the protection of a cold frame for a year, sizeable bulbs will be produced within two or three years.

GLORIOUS GLADIOLI

Gladioli are very useful summer-flowering subjects, producing bold, brightly coloured spikes of blossom during late summer. The large-flowered hybrids are ideal for cutting, while the smaller kinds are more suited to general border decoration. Both kinds can be planted where they are to flower immediately the danger of frost has passed. For an informal setting they can be planted at random, but if they are being grown

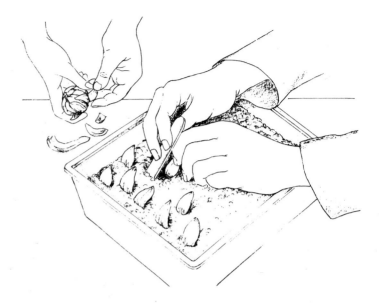

Fig. 5a   Inserting plump lily scales into a tray of compost.

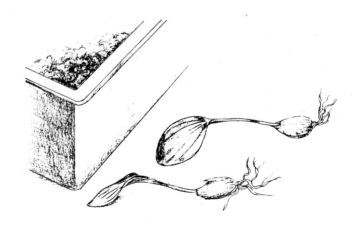

Fig. 5b   Sprouted lily scales six to eight months later.

for cutting alone it is easier to accommodate them in rows.

There are many varieties of the large-flowered hybrids available and the gardener can divide these roughly into two main groups according to their usefulness: those that are good for general garden decoration and those which, in addition, are well suited for cutting. General garden varieties are dominated by the lovely red 'Cordula' and 'Hunting Song', together with the rich orange 'Nicole' and delicate pink 'Friendship'. It is worth looking out for the bright yellow 'Flower Song', 'Aldebaran', 'Nova Lux' and 'Groene Specht', as well as the pure white 'Teach In' and 'White Friendship'. 'Hunting Song', 'Nova Lux', 'Friendship' and 'Teach In' are also good for cutting. However, where this is the primary concern, then the lovely orange 'Saxony' and 'Peter Pears' should be tried. Do not neglect either the charming pink 'My Love' or pink and apricot 'Praha', for these are amongst the finest varieties of this popular cut flower.

The shorter growing kinds are mostly the earlier flowering *nanus* group. These are invaluable in the mixed border, being inexpensive, reliable and rarely growing more than 60 cm in height. Most gardeners who have grown these wonderful little plants agree that the best variety is 'Nymph'. It blossoms for a longer period than almost any other, can be planted more sparingly, and yet provides the same effect. As a bonus its beautiful white blossoms with a delicate crimson shading are perfect for cutting. 'Blushing Bride' looks very similar but is not as free-flowering, while 'The Bride', although vigorous, never yields the same quantity of blossom as 'Nymph'. 'Ackerman' is an old variety with orange-red flowers, while those of 'Amanda Mahy' are deep pink with mauve internal splashes. 'Peach Blossom' is an exceptional pink kind, which although rather aged, has yet to be surpassed in its own colour range.

All these small-growing gladioli flower from mid-summer onwards outdoors, although there is no reason why they cannot be planted in pots the previous autumn for cool greenhouse cultivation and early spring flowering. Ordinarily these and the large-flowered hybrids are planted during spring so that their emerging spears of foliage miss damaging late frosts. The corms should be covered by about their own depth in soil and as soon as young shoots appear through the soil, those that are going to require staking should receive a cane. As growth develops they must be tied into their supports, especially when the flower spike comes into evidence. Providing that they are kept weed-free, gladioli grown on a free-draining soil present no cultural difficulties, especially if planted in a sunny sheltered position.

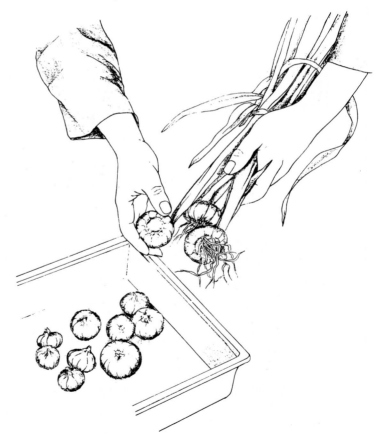

Fig. 6 Gladioli – when the foliage has died back it is removed and the corms are prepared for storage.

The lovely *Narcissus cyclamineus* 'Jenny' associates happily with orange-flowered crown imperials, *Fritillaria imperialis* 'Aurora'.

When flowering has finished, the plants should be encouraged to continue growing until the frost blackens the foliage. While it is not wise to feed the plants during this period, it is as well to see that the foliage is kept fresh and green and that the plants have sufficient moisture. Once the frost has done its work, then the corms must be lifted and dried prior to storing in a cool airy place. Spread the corms out in trays (Fig.6) or on a small frame covered with wire netting to allow air to circulate and dry them off properly. All blackened foliage should be cut off near to the top of each corm, and the corm inverted so that any lingering moisture can drain out of the end of the hollow stem. When the corms have dried off completely, all the remaining soil can be rubbed off and any decaying or superfluous foliage removed.

Dusting the corms with flowers of sulphur is a useful precaution against storage moulds before they are suspended in nets in a cool, but frost-free, place. Regular inspections for signs of decay should be made during the winter months and any suspect corms must be removed, but most will remain sound and healthy for planting the following spring.

A SUMMER SPECTACULAR

Tigridias

Gorgeous blossoms in the summer garden are not just the perogative of lilies and gladioli. The tiger flowers or tigridias are equally flamboyant. These have exotic blossoms which look like tropical butterflies at rest amongst their rigid sword-shaped foliage. Individual blossoms are transitory, lasting but a single day. However, so many are produced that a continuous show can be expected throughout the summer. Each flower is three-petalled with a single strong background colour, the centre of each flower being a different hue with bold orange or yellow splashes. Planted during late

spring they should appear through the soil at around the time the last frost has passed. They are rather like small gladioli when they first appear, but emerge in small clumps rather than as individual fans of leaves. Although easy going in any soil, they do require an open sunny position if they are to prosper. Even the dappled shade caused by a nearby tree or shrub is sufficient to impair their flowering.

Acidanthera

Acidanthera are a similar proposition, especially in cooler northern parts where the bulbs do not come into flower until around the time of the first frost. Their blossoms are exquisite, being borne in slender spires: rather like a gladiolus, but all are richly fragrant and pure white with a deep purple-red throat. Attaining a height of 75–90 cm (2½–3 ft), they grow well in the open ground and look rather better there than in pots. Many gardeners find that it is a good compromise to plunge the pots containing the corms into the open ground where they can develop naturally, just bringing them in if frost threatens before all the blossoms have opened. I have grown these little gems in aquatic planting baskets and then removed them from the border if necessary at flowering time. The baskets being of a lattice-work construction enable the soil within to be as moist as that outside. Another advantage is that you can always be sure of removing all the bulbs if you are using this planting technique merely as a means of ensuring early clearance of a bed. Both acidanthera and tigridia are doubtfully hardy and so best lifted and stored for the winter in the same way as advocated for gladioli.

Sparaxis

Similar techniques have to be adopted if sparaxis is to be cultivated successfully outdoors in any but the mildest parts of the country. Popularly known as harlequin flowers, these are natives of South Africa;

they grow from tiny corms and have delicate brightly coloured blossoms held aloft on slender wand-like stems. Usually of a pink or pastel colour, the harlequin flowers enjoy a sunny well drained spot on the rock garden. They can often be successfully grown in such a position when planted directly into the soil, but for other places the use of a container which can be plunged into the soil is essential. Unlike acidanthera where the problem is attributable to late flowering, with sparaxis it is associated with early emergence. The corms break into growth very quickly after planting and the emerging spears of growth are vulnerable to frost damage.

Ixia

It is a similar story with the corn lilies or ixias. These are also natives of southern Africa, but are more brash and with brightly coloured starry blossoms on wiry stems. As the flowers only open in full sun, during the afternoon and early evening, careful positioning in the garden is vital. Ixias are essentially plants for sunny areas, although in more hostile climates they do respond to pot cultivation. Their principal requirements are plenty of light and a free-draining soil or compost.

Eucomis

The pineapple flower, *Eucomis bicolor*, enjoys the same sort of conditions. In sheltered areas it can become a permanent resident in the garden if protected during winter with a layer of ashes or dried bracken. In localities where it is a doubtful outdoor proposition, eucomis can be treated successfully as an annual inhabitant of the mixed border. It is a most striking and unusual character which seems to have no qualms about being moved back indoors for the winter. When frost threatens, merely lift the bulbs and pack them into boxes of peat in a frost-free place.

Eucomis is one of the most bizarre of the summer-flowering bulbs, producing strange flower heads which at a distance resemble a pineapple fruit. The closely packed star-shaped flowers are greenish-yellow, the whole spike topped with a tuft of leaves. If left to their own devices, the flower heads will yield a heavy crop of attractive rounded seed pods. When cut and dried, the seed that is produced can be used to increase stock, although detachable bulbils are produced around the parent bulb from time to time.

Crocosmia

Crocosmia always reproduces freely. This is the genus of plant which now contains all those formerly known as garden montbretias. The name *Montbretia* is only used for the rare *Montbretia laxiflora*. All the cottage garden montbretias are now correctly varieties of *Crocosmia crocosmiiflora*. These include named sorts like the lemon-yellow 'Citronella' and orange-scarlet 'His Majesty'. Although commonly associated with Victorian gardens, and with a reputation for being invasive, the modern varieties like the bright red 'Spitfire' are well behaved and very hardy.

Galtonia

So too is the hardy summer hyacinth or galtonia, a majestic plant that drips its creamy-white bells from tall elegant stems all summer long. This should be established amongst low-growing shrubs where its blossoms can seek the sunlight, but its unruly foliage can be disguised by their dense leafy growth. Apart from the popular *Galtonia candicans*, there is a greenish-flowered species known as *G. princeps*. Both reproduce freely from seed.

Ornithogalum

Chincherinchee, *Ornithogalum thyrsoides*, blooms at about the same time with upright spires of starry white

29

Narcissus provide a carpet beneath an established magnolia. Sufficient space is left close by to prevent competition from the roots.

Chionodoxa gigantea is the perfect small spring flowering bulb for colonizing the bare soil beneath flowering shrubs.

flowers. Superb for cutting, this easily grown exotic from southern Africa is doubtfully hardy and benefits from lifting and storing during the winter months. Although of a somewhat formal appearance, chincherinchee is at ease in most situations, looking especially fine when established amongst evergreen ground cover like common periwinkle, provided that it is in full sun. Apart from its versatility in the border, the chincherinchee and its interesting cousin *O. arabicum*, respond well to tub and pot culture.

Ranunculus

Ranunculus on the other hand are essentially plants of the open border, much preferring a cool root run and tolerating a little shade. The turban ranunculus are technically neither bulbs nor corms, although their claw-like rootstocks are dealt with almost exclusively by the bulb trade. Unfortunately, these strange little rootstocks tend to cause all kinds of confusion for the newcomer to gardening, especially with regard to the correct way to plant them. Bury them just beneath the surface of the soil with the points of the claws downwards. Ranunculus produce typical glossy green buttercup-like foliage and attractive, almost globular,

heads of flower in myriad brilliant colours. Although a relative of the buttercup, turban ranunculus are well behaved and not at all invasive. They can be used freely for brightening up the border, but are grown by most gardeners for cutting.

Anemone

Anemones can also be useful for cutting, especially the single De Caen and semi-double St Brigid strains. These are available in many bright colours and can be planted at regular intervals from early spring onwards to ensure a succession of blossoms. Specialist bulb suppliers sometimes list both De Caen and St Brigid type anemones by cultivar names. When available these are superb, especially the rich deep purple-blue 'Mr Fokker' and fiery red 'Hollandia'. The black or brown raisin-like rootstock popularly known as a corm, is botanically a tuber, and by virtue of this fact is able to expand in the soil, so once you have planted anemones they are a permanent feature. However, persuading freshly purchased tubers to sprout can be difficult unless you soak them in water overnight. All the sound tubers are then planted about their own depth beneath the surface of the soil.

3

AUTUMN AND WINTER COLOUR

Few gardeners exploit the diversity of bulbs that are available for autumn and winter flowering, especially the early autumn flowered subjects, for these have to be planted during late summer at a time when the garden is demanding and the floral display still good. Thoughts rarely turn towards an autumn display at this time and the result is many good plants are not exploited as well as they could be.

NAKED LADIES AND AUTUMN CROCUS

Colchicums are one of the most popular autumn-flowering subjects. Some people confuse them with autumn crocus, for they have the appearance of a giant crocus when in flower. Others call them naked ladies because they produce their handsome lilac, purple or white blossoms before their bulky glossy green foliage appears. There are numerous kinds, but the lilac-flowered *Colchicum speciosum* is the most widely available, together with its white form *album* and the fully double lilac 'Waterlily'. Colchicums, apart from being invaluable plants for the garden can usually be persuaded to flower indoors without planting. Being sizeable bulbs with a large food reserve, it is common practice to stand them on a window ledge without soil and let them blossom. Provided that the bulbs are planted immediately after flowering they will not come to any harm.

The true autumn crocus is typified by the meadow saffron, *Crocus sativus*, a small-flowered species with delicate rosy purple flowers. *Crocus speciosus* is very similar, but has yielded some superb cultivars, amongst them the blue 'Oxonian', pale violet-blue 'Pollux' and lavender 'Cassiope'. All are planted during late summer and flower from early autumn until severe winter weather strikes. This also applies to *Sternbergia lutea*, an increasingly popular bright yellow flowered crocus-like plant. Apart from its usefulness as a garden plant, it is invaluable for pot work in the unheated greenhouse.

AUTUMN EXOTICS

Amongst the late summer- and autumn-flowering bulbs are a number of hardy, but exotic looking beauties. These do not associate readily with many of our popular garden subjects and so are better planted as autumn highlights in different parts of the garden. Most will only mix happily with plants like phormium, yucca and cordyline, characters which are able to give the temperate garden a touch of the tropical.

Nerine

Amongst these is the hardy nerine, *Nerine bowdenii*. This is a handsome exotic-looking bulbous plant which despite its appearance is perfectly hardy and flowers freely when planted in a situation to its liking. A south- or west-facing aspect is preferable, the base of

Despite their formal aspect, late spring flowering tulips associate happily with the tangled vegetation of a cottage garden.

Tulips and old fashioned border plants provide the flavour of a bygone era in this spring garden.

a wall being ideal. It likes a good baking from the sun, yet at the same time will not prosper in very dry impoverished soil. Delicate rosy pink flowers are produced on strong stems before the leaves appear, first opening during late summer and in open weather persisting almost until Christmas. The bulbs often take a while to settle down before flowering, preferring to grow in crowded conditions where they can stand shoulder to shoulder.

Amaryllis

The hardy amaryllis is a similar proposition. Not to be confused with the florist's amaryllis, *Amaryllis belladonna* is a superb short-growing pink-flowered species that flowers during early autumn. The trumpet-shaped blossoms are produced on short stout stems before the characteristic strap-like foliage appears. Like the nerine, this is a bulb for the base of a wall.

Fig. 7 Snowdrops are best lifted and divided 'in green', immediately after flowering.

Crinum

So too are the giant crinums, but unlike most other autumn-flowering subjects these are best planted during spring. Giants of the bulb world, *Crinum powellii* and its progeny have bulbs which vary in size from a tennis ball to a field swede. They also have very distinctive long necks and bold fleshy strap-shaped leaves that never seem to go completely dormant. Crinums produce umbels of large trumpet-shaped blossoms on stout erect stems. In the original hybrid these are a pale pink colour, while in *album* they are white, and in 'Krelagei' intense rose-pink.

Snowdrops, Aconites and Snowflakes

Snowdrops and winter aconites are the harbingers of spring, twinkling through a mantle of snow and giving a hint of floral pleasures to come. Hardy and reliable characters, they will grow almost anywhere and increase freely every year. Apart from cheering up the garden in early spring, they can be grown in places where few other plants will prosper, carpeting the ground beneath tall trees and stealing light and moisture before they awake. Both naturalize freely in a grassy sward and can be planted liberally amongst ground cover plants. Snowdrops peeping through a dark green carpet of periwinkle or scrambling ivy present a picture of cool stark beauty. Scattered amongst the richly coloured stems of red barked dogwood they are sheer delight. So is a golden halo of aconites around prickly holly. Such delights, however, need not be confined to the garden alone, for snowdrops and aconites flourish in tubs and pots. Try them in a container on the patio, or invest in a few to brighten up a window box.

Winter aconites, *Eranthis hyemalis*, have sparkling, starry, golden blossoms surrounded by a bright green ruff of foliage. They grow from small dark tubers which can be planted at any time during the autumn, although if you have some that you would like to move they are best lifted and divided during spring, immediately after flowering. In a happy environment aconites seed themselves freely, forming a dense carpet of green foliage which persists until early summer. Snowdrops are equally amenable and readily divided and transplanted 'in green', that is after they have flowered and yet are still growing freely (Fig. 7). For conventional planting they are best purchased as bulbs in the early autumn, well before growth commences.

The common snowdrop is *Galanthus nivalis*, a charming little plant with pendant tear-like blossoms with snow-white petals splashed with green. It has given rise to many varieties, the majority of which are only of botanical interest, but a number are very garden worthy, especially the donkey-eared snowdrop, 'Scharlokii', a curious plant discovered in a German garden during the last century. In this variety the two green spathes of the flower, instead of being united, have become divided and lengthened, thus protruding like rabbits' or donkeys' ears behind the blossom to give a somewhat comical appearance.

The varieties *flavescens* and *lutescens* are characterized by yellow instead of green markings on the inner segments, while 'Viridapicis' sports a bold green marking on the tip of each outer segment. This is a strong grower which reproduces freely in a moist situation, conditions which are ideal for 'Flore Pleno', a much loved and easily grown fully double form of the traditional snowdrop. Not all varieties have physical attributes which separate them clearly from their brothers; a number differ markedly in their flowering period. Typical of these is *reginae-olgae*, a little gem that thrusts up typical snowdrop blossom during early to mid-autumn, well in advance of its foliage. The closely allied species *G. corycensis* follows during late autumn and early winter, while the late flowering selection *G. nivalis* 'April Fool' hangs on to its flowers until mid-spring.

Snowflakes resemble closely the snowdrops, and are versatile plants freely available, but which are rarely exploited. The best loved and most frequently encoun-tered is the summer snowflake, *Leucojum aestivum*, a handsome snowdrop-like plant about 60 cm (2 ft) high with pendulous white bell-like blossoms bearing conspicuous green markings. These flower later than any of the snowdrops, usually from mid-spring until mid-summer. The spring snowflake, *L. vernuum*, is very similar but much more useful, blossoming during late winter and early spring alongside its illustrious cousins. It has much larger flowers, but despite this is neat and compact, rarely exceeding 20 cm (8 in) in height, even in the choice form *carpathicum* in which the snow-white blossoms are conspicuously marked with yellow. Both enjoy a cool moist root run and are well suited to poolside culture.

Crocus, Squills and Iris

Crocus provide really early colour and can be grown almost anywhere without difficulty. The large flowered Dutch types or 'fat boys' can be a little fussy, preferring life in an open border rather than in grass. They are available in a wide range of colours, from the golden-yellow of 'Yellow Mammoth' to the purple of 'Remembrance' and white of 'Joan of Arc'. However, it is the so-called species crocus that are the best value, especially the little multi-flowered cultivars of *Crocus chrysanthus*. Flowering in late winter, these are ideal for naturalizing in grass. The blue and white 'Ladykiller' is quite breathtaking, a splendid companion for the pure white 'Snow Bunting' and dusky 'Zwanenburg Bronze'.

The scillas or squills are equally lovely. Tiny early-flowering bulbs that flourish almost anywhere, carpeting the ground in a sea of blue. There are many different kinds of early flowering squills, but none more lovely or versatile than *Scilla tubergeniana*. A hardy little gem that flowers from late winter until early spring with delicate pale blue blossoms, each with a dark blue stripe. An excellent plant when grown indoors in a pan, it is equally happy in the garden, tolerating the most hostile winter weather. It forms a dense carpet planted beneath shrubs or it can be used to

Spring flowering bulbs produce a floral carpet beneath these large trees before their leaf canopy closes in.

Mixed large flowered daffodils provide early spring colour beside a rushing stream before the waterside plants awaken.

colonize grassy banks and similar difficult areas. *Scilla sibirica* is just as prolific, but flowers a little later, with more pendant blossoms of intense Prussian-blue. This is ideal for naturalizing, seeding itself freely and very quickly forming sizeable colonies. There is also an improved kind called 'Spring Beauty' which is of the same intense blue, as well as a pure white selection which is sometimes encountered. While not a true squill, the striped squill *Puschkinia scilloides* is often mistaken for one, and is a striking plant with attractive spires of pale blue blossoms conspicuously marked with deep greenish-blue. This is one of the hardiest and most successful dwarf bulbs for damp places, although just as happy when confined to a free-draining pocket on the rock garden.

The dark blue *Iris reticulata* is an amiable companion. The commonest of the dwarf bulbous iris species, it provides a striking picture during early spring along with *I. danfordiae*. Of all the *I. reticulata* cultivars the soft blue 'Joyce' and 'Harmony' are the most reliable, although the plum coloured 'J.S.Dijt' should not be overlooked. *Iris danfordiae* is a dwarf yellow flowering kind, while the allied *I. vartani alba* is a *reticulata* type with blossoms of cool icy-white.

4

USING BULBS IN BEDS AND BORDERS

Until recent years one of the most popular uses for bulbs was in a formal arrangement with spring bedding plants. Their versatility was not as widely appreciated as now, certainly not in the field of naturalizing. While more formal plantings have gone into decline, they are nevertheless still an important aspect of gardening.

FORMAL PLANTING

There are many different methods of utilizing bulbs in a formal arrangement, tulips, narcissus, hyacinths and crocus being the most versatile kinds to use. However, before we consider what can be done, it is important to look at the soil and see what is a practical proposition.

On a newly cultivated site narcissus and crocus are likely to be the most reliable, while tulips and hyacinths respond better on well cultivated land or that which is light and free-draining. Soil conditions are of paramount importance in establishing a successful display, for variable structure and nutrient levels lead to irregular growth, a disaster in a formal planting scheme. As formal bulb displays are usually only of annual duration, much can be done to regularly improve soil conditions, so that after several years of cultivation any suitable variety of bulb can be arranged in any configuration.

All bulbs benefit from a free-draining soil that is rich in organic matter. For formal plantings the structure should be good and the medium friable so that the bulbs can be planted at the appropriate depths and dis-

tances without restriction. A well prepared soil that is raked to a fine tilth and is weed-free is the ideal. On this the design can be laid down by using a generous quantity of sand to mark the outline. Using strings and pegs, and if necessary a large set square, the outline can very accurately be established. Once this has been done, bulbs can be planted systematically, using a short cane the length of the required planting distance as a marker. The bulbs are then arranged accurately (if guesswork is allowed to creep in the resulting display can look patchy). Similarly, accurate planting depths

Fig. 8 Always use a trowel rather than a dibber when planting bulbs.

The blue starry blossoms of *Anemone blanda* peep out from beneath an army of daffodils. Both naturalize happily together.

Although related to snowdrops, snowflakes are much larger. They are ideal bulbs for heavy, wet soil.

must be observed if heights are to be even. To help achieve this, use a proper bulb-planting trowel. This has different levels marked in it, so that it is possible to plant bulbs speedily and accurately to a predetermined depth (Fig.8).

In order to produce a really first-class display the design should be drawn out on graph paper well before you purchase your bulbs. The quantities can then be accurately determined. Inevitably you will require significantly more than you imagined, but it is important to plant the requisite number or the full impact at flowering time will be lost. It is also essential to study the flowering periods of different varieties. It may sound ideal to plant red tulips and white tulips in close proximity, but if their flowering is not synchronized, the display will be a disaster. Before planning a formal arrangement it is best to look at a living display in your area. Careful observation will reveal which varieties flower together. Do not rely upon a catalogue description, for different varieties behave in different ways when grown in the north or the south. Varieties that flower together in the south may well flower a week apart in the north. In other words, you really need to plan your display a year ahead, unless you have very sound local knowledge of how certain varieties behave in your district.

When putting a design together, try to be adventurous. Large blocks of colour are fine, but they become a little tedious after several seasons. By virtue of their method of growth, most bulbs respond to integration into quite complicated designs. Even floral lettering can be arranged with smaller bulbs like scilla and crocus. This is not difficult to do, for all that is required is the shape of the finished letter or motif cut out of a large piece of cardboard. This is secured to the ground and the bulbs are planted within the large stencil-like cut-out. Once the bulbs are in the soil, the cut-out is removed. All kinds of imaginative designs can be arranged using this technique, not only with letters, but a series of shapes as well. It is not always essential to plant formal designs in bare earth. Very effective arrangements can be contrived in close mown grass, the green background being a perfect foil.

BULBS AND BEDDING

Bulbs have long been associated with spring bedding plants. Many parks put on commendable displays of bulbs and spring-bedding plants even in these times of financial stringency. The combination of blue forget-me-nots and pink tulips is an unforgettable spectacle, but one which takes care and patience to bring off successfully. Accurate planting plans are necessary because the bulbs have to go in first, the bedding plants being planted over the top of them. So you are effectively putting together a design in two stages.

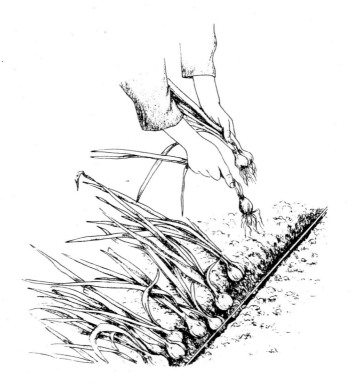

Fig. 9a Spring-flowering bulbs, which have been removed to make way for summer-bedding plants, are carefully heeled in a shallow trench.

Mark out the areas to be occupied by the bulbs using short canes and strings. Plant the bulbs at their carefully measured distances leaving the strings and canes in place until the wall-flowers or forget-me-nots have been planted over the top. Take care not to disturb the bulbs underneath when planting. If you are not too confident about coming over the top with bedding plants, then plant the bulbs deeper than normal. Both tulips and narcissus respond favourably to deeper planting, most varieties being able to perform well at twice the normal recommended depth. Provided all the bulbs are planted at the same depth, they will attain a uniform height. The only discrepancies likely in height are then between different varieties.

BULBS FOR BEDS AND BORDERS

The diversity of shape, colour, fragrance and habit amongst the bulbs that can be used in beds and borders is legion. There is truly something for everyone. Even when looking at stiffly formal and regimented bulbs like hyacinths there is wide variation, particularly in colour. Gardeners who use hyacinths regularly for bedding tend to grow well tried varieties like 'Queen of the Whites', the primrose-yellow 'City of Haarlem', 'King of the Blues' and maybe the lovely pink 'Princess Irene'. However, there are other interesting colours worth trying, including 'Tubergen's Scarlet' and the salmon-orange 'Cinderella'. Recently multiflora hyacinths have come to the fore and these are likely to be seen more frequently in future bedding schemes. Although their flower spikes are not as solid and formal as those of the ordinary hyacinth, they are more

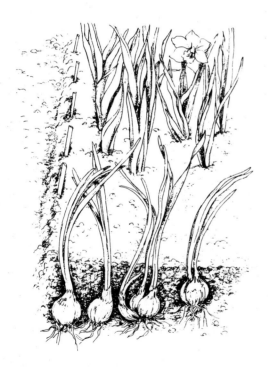

Fig. 9b The bulbs can be heeled in close together without coming to any harm.

Fig. 9c Carefully firm in, leaving the foliage to continue building up the bulbs.

The giant football-like flower heads of the ornamental onions create a spectacle in the late spring garden.

numerous and give a far more economical display, the bulbs being planted at twice the usual distance and yet providing a similar visual impact.

Tulips can be used more economically if multi-flowered varieties are planted. The best one to grow is the lovely red variety of *Tulipa praestans* called 'Fusilier'. This often carries four or five large flowers on a stem and unlike other tulips is particularly amenable to heavy soil. Of the traditional kinds the groups or divisions most commonly grown for bedding are the single early, triumph, lily-flowered and Darwin tulips. All are easy to grow in an open sunny situation in a free-draining soil. Recommending varieties is folly, because there are literally hundreds and every gardener has his favourites. All those that are commonly offered by the bulb merchant or garden centre are likely to have proved popular and reliable.

The same applies with narcissus, although several divisions of the classification are better for display work than others. These include the trumpet narcissi or daffodils – old favourites like 'Golden Harvest' and 'Kingscourt' – as well as the large-cupped varieties like 'Carlton' and 'Galway'. Some of the tougher double varieties like 'Texas' are good bedding kinds, but many

of the newer sorts are not very weatherproof. This is not the case with the *N. cyclamineus* hybrids which are bold, tough and reliable daffodils, a little shorter and smaller-flowered than the traditional kinds, but capable of a stunning display. 'Jenny' is creamy white, and both 'Peeping Tom' and 'February Gold' deep yellow.

All the bulbs mentioned here are tough and reliable, but only the narcissus can usually be used for a second season, and then only when very carefully looked after. The critical period in their life is directly after flowering, the time when the space that they occupy is ready to be prepared for summer bedding. If carefully lifted and then heeled into a corner of the vegetable plot they should develop satisfactorily (Fig. 9a–c). The important thing is to avoid disturbing them, so that their foliage does not deteriorate. It is this that will build up the bulbs for next year and ensure a satisfactory display.

While many gardeners advocate this practice for tulips and hyacinths as well, in reality it is not practicable. Ideally, treat them as annuals and buy afresh next year. That way, not only do you save labour, but you almost certainly guarantee a first-class display as well.

5

BRIGHTENING WINDOW BOXES AND PLANTERS

Bulbs are well suited to cultivation in containers and window boxes, but their success depends mainly upon two factors. They must be situated in an open sunny position and planted in a compost that is moisture retentive.

COMPOSTS AND CARE

The compost is especially critical, for an ill-conceived mixture that is either too wet or not moisture-retentive enough can spell disaster. It is true that if good quality bulbs are purchased, there is a good quality embryo flower inside, but it can only achieve its full potential if growing conditions are favourable. Drainage is also very important, for few bulbs will enjoy sitting in the wet, but equally a fast-draining compost that dries out quickly is undesirable.

Some gardeners believe that they can make up a suitable compost themselves by taking ordinary garden soil, sand, peat and fertilizer, and mixing it together. It probably looks good, but it is unsterilized and contains unknown levels of plant foods. Weed seeds will germinate readily and proliferate and you will probably be plagued with slugs and snails. Such a compost, generally made on the grounds of economy, is anything but economical. What is needed is a good quality compost like John Innes No.3. This is made from sterilized loam, sand and peat with John Innes base fertilizer added. Having a loam base it is excellent, for if neces-

sary you can use a liquid feed without any fear of the compost structure deteriorating as eventually happens with peat, or peat and sand-based soil-less types.

Soil-less composts are a poor substitute for the John Innes kinds. They are inferior on two counts; they are relatively short-lived in terms of plant foods, and without the soil component their structure deteriorates badly. Few bulbs grow naturally in such a peaty organic medium, so unless plenty of grit is added many of them will not prosper. The only merit that can be claimed for soil-less compost when growing bulbs is its lighter weight which can be important where window boxes are involved. When weight is a factor, it is wise to be very selective about the bulbs that you grow. Daffodils, snowdrops and squills seem to enjoy soil-less compost, but other popular sorts like tulips and hyacinths are less enthusiastic about it.

One of the major problems with planters and window boxes is keeping them moist during warm or windy weather, especially if you are out at work all day and there is nobody to keep an eye on them. So introduce a soil additive such as perlite or arcillite. These should be incorporated into your compost at about a quarter by volume. Being inert they do not affect the acidity, alkalinity or nutrient content of the compost. What they do is to enable moisture to be absorbed when you are watering, the particles releasing it back into the soil as it dries out. This enables containers to be watered less frequently and overcomes to some extent the adverse effect of alternate drying and dampening which can cause stress to bulbs of all kinds.

Apart from compost quality, the other major factor in container cultivation is drainage. Adequate drainage facilities are essential. A waterlogged container will be the end of your bulb display. If you have an attractive container with no proper drainage hole, then it is necessary to put a generous layer of shingle or broken crocks in the bottom before introducing the compost. This is not really adequate, but it is better than nothing and you can usually get away with growing most flower bulbs without too much difficulty. However, drainage material occupies the space that should be taken by compost, so many bulbs cannot be recommended for small or shallow containers.

EARLY SPRING COLOUR

The choice of bulbs for a spring display is wide and varied, for almost all except the tall-growing kinds are well suited to container conditions. These are merely excluded because of their vulnerability to wind. It is wise to choose one part of the spring season for your display: trying to create a succession of blossoms is difficult to achieve satisfactorily. Hyacinths are a natural choice as they associate well visually with a formal setting. All the popular varieties are satisfactory, but as they have slightly variable flowering periods only use one kind in each container. Tulips are ideal for containers and window boxes, especially the so-called botanical tulips derived from *Tulipa kaufmanniana*, *T. eichleri*, *T. fosterians* and *T. greigii*. These are all compact, early flowering, and very wind-resistant. The red multi-headed *Tulipa praestans* is another favourite for this kind of display, being especially useful for mixing with the starry blue glory of the snow, *Chionodoxa luciliae*. Grape hyacinths can also be used. The best is *Muscari armeniacum*, which is perfect when used for filling a container on its own.

Some of the large modern daffodil varieties are rather heavy in appearance when used in window boxes. Especially the fully double types and the new split corona kinds. The delicate little *Narcissus cyclamineus* varieties are much better and most flower earlier than conventional types. They are bold little daffodils with petals that are laid back and surround prominent, narrow trumpets. 'Jenny' is a lovely pale creamy-white sort, while 'February Gold' and 'Peeping Tom' are the pick of the yellows. The dainty little yellow multi-headed 'Tête-à-Tête' is closely allied and well suited to the smaller container. Crocus are also useful for small tubs and make first-class subjects for old-fashioned strawberry pots. The so-called Dutch crocus like 'Remembrance' and 'Yellow Mammoth' are preferable to the smaller flowered *Crocus chrysanthus* varieties. Anemones are attractive plants for container work, especially the dwarf blue daisy-like *Anemone blanda*. This has many good varieties in pastel shades and forms a solid carpet of foliage and blossom in the first year. Scillas are amongst the most reliable spring-flowering bulbs. *Scilla sibirica* and the improved 'Spring Beauty' look like miniature bluebells, while *S. tubergeniana* sports pale blue flowers with darker stripes very early in the year. While not advocating a variable flowering period for container grown bulbs, there is great merit in planting late winter-flowering *S. tubergeniana* amongst late spring-blooming wallflowers.

BULBS OF SUMMER

Bulbs are not often the main consideration when planting window boxes and planters for a summer display. Bedding plants are usually the order of the day and quite rightly so, for few bulbs can equal the intensity of colour and length of season offered by modern bedding plants. The only case for introducing bulbs is that most of the smaller summer blooming kinds are easier to manage in a container, such as the lovely white flowered acidanthera, sparaxis and of course ixia. None could be considered to be good value when colour is the main requirement; the only summer-flowering subject that could approach these demands is the canna. Not really a bulb, rather a swollen rootstock that is part of the stock in trade of the bulb merchant,

Montbretia has always been considered invasive. Now renamed *Crocosmia*, modern cultivars like 'Vulcan' are restrained, and yet colourful.

Lilies, like 'Grand Commander' prosper in a rich, damp, leafy soil in a dappled shade.

the canna is a first-class plant for containers, but too tall for a window box. With bold tropical looking leaves, rather like those of a banana plant the cannas give an exotic look to the most mundane yard or patio. They have either green or purple-bronze foliage and spikes of almost gladiolus-like blossoms in vivid reds, oranges and yellow. Usually available from early spring onwards as rootstocks, they should be started in pots of a good potting compost and given frost-free protection. They grow quickly and can be planted in their summer home when all danger of frost has passed. Like gladioli, the roots are lifted after the first

sharp frost and stored in a cool dark place. Do not string them up in a net though, for they easily dry out. A deep box of peat is the best thing to keep them in.

Lilies can be grown in containers, provided you deal with them in the same way as recommended for the house or greenhouse. Choose reliable sorts like the Mid-Century hybrids and ensure that they do not go short of water. Again these are not well suited to window-box culture. During the summer you are rather restricted if you have a window box, so stick to summer bedding, maybe interspersing it with a few bulbs of sparaxis or ixia.

SELECTED RECOMMENDED BULBS FOR CONTAINERS AND WINDOW BOXES

Bulbs can be planted much closer together in containers than in the garden, simply ensuring that they do not touch each other or the sides of the container. In single layer planting, place bulbs at same depth as if planting in the open garden, normally 12-15 cm (5-6 in) deep for large bulbs, 5-8 cm (2-3 in) for smaller bulbs. For a really concentrated dislay, bulbs can be planted into two or three layers, as long as they are not planted directly over each other. Always water well after planting, and provide protection from frost.

Bulb	Colour	Height	
Anemone de Caen St. Brigid	Various	25-30 cm	(10–12 in)
Chinodoxa luciliae	Bright blue	10-15 cm	(4–6 in)
Colchicum species/hybrids	Various	15-20 cm	(6–8 in)
Crocus (autumn-flowering species)	Various	7.5 cm	(3 in)
Crocus (spring-flowering species)	Various	7.5 cm	(3 in)
Crocus (Dutch hybrids)	Various	7.5 cm	(3 in)
Cyclamen coum	Purplish–pink	10 cm	(4 in)
Cyclamen neapolitanum	Rose–pink	10 cm	(4 in)
Cyclamen repandum	Lilac–pink	10 cm	(4 in)

Bulb	Colour	Height	
Eranthis hyemalis	Golden yellow	7.5 cm	(3 in)
Erythronium dens-canis	Various	10-15 cm	(4–6 in)
Galanthus elwesii	White/green	17.5 cm	(7 in)
Galanthus nivalis	White/green	15 cm	(6 in)
Hyacinth named varieties	Various	30 cm	(12 in)
Iris danfordiae	Yellow	7.5 cm	(3 in)
Iris reticulata varieties	Various	10-15 cm	(4–6 in)
Muscari armeniacum	Blue	15-20 cm	(6–8 in)
Muscari botryoides album	White	15-25 cm	(6–10 in)
Narcissus cyclamineus 'Jack Snipe'	White/Yellow	22.5 cm	(9 in)
N.c. 'February Gold'	Yellow	30 cm	(12 in)
N.c. 'Jenny'	White	25 cm	(10 in)
N.c. 'Tete-a-Tete'	Yellow	20 cm	(8 in)
N.jonquilla	Yellow	30 cm	(12 in)
N.triandrus albus	Creamy white	17.5 cm	(7 in)
Puschkinia libanotica	Light blue	15 cm	(6 in)
Scilla sibirica	Dark blue	10 cm	(4 in)
Scilla tubergeniana	Light blue	10 cm	(4 in)
Tulipa eichleri	Red	20 cm	(8 in)
T.praestens 'Fusilier'	Red	25 cm	(10 in)
T.kaufmanniana hybrids	Various	10-25 cm	(4–10 in)
T.fosteriana hybrids	Various	20-40 cm	(8–16 in)
T.greigii hybrids	Various	22.5-50 cm	(9–20 in)
Single Early tulips	Various	25-60 cm	(10–24 in)
Double Early tulips	Various	25-30 cm	(10–12 in)

6

BULBS IN POTS AND BOWLS

BULBS FOR CHRISTMAS FLOWERING

One of the benefits of growing bulbs in pots and bowls is that you have a measure of control over their life cycle, and consequently their flowering period. It is a tremendous morale booster in the dark days of winter, when you can arrange to witness the emergence of the sweetly-scented blossoms of the paper-white narcissus or the sentinel-like columns of brightly coloured hyacinths. With consistent cultivation it is not difficult to have a number of different bulbs in full flower at Christmas providing that you follow a few basic cultural rules and select suitable varieties of properly prepared bulbs.

It is essential to start thinking about Christmas-flowering bulbs during late summer. Your choice is a little limited for really early flowering, because only hyacinths respond properly to pre-preparation and the varieties of narcissus or tulip that can be used are limited. However, amongst the wealth of early flowering bulbs like snowdrops, crocus, chionodoxa and scilla there are many kinds that can be persuaded to flower early by being afforded some protection. Nevertheless, early planting is essential, for all require between ten and fourteen weeks in cool conditions plunged in a frame or bed of peat or ashes outside. This enables them to establish a good root system before being subjected to an unnaturally high temperature. If successful establishment is not achieved, the plants will often collapse when taken out into the warmth and light. It depends upon variety, but it takes most bulbs

at least three or four weeks to reach flowering stage from being brought inside, so for successful Christmas flowering all bulbs must be planted by early autumn.

Use bulb fibre, especially if you are planting your bulbs in a bowl or container that does not have drainage holes. Bulb fibre is a coarse medium, largely consisting of fibrous peat moss, but with charcoal and oyster shell grit incorporated to keep it sweet. It contains virtually no nutrients, so the bulbs are largely dependent upon their own resources. Small bulbs like snowdrops and chionodoxa are better off in a straightforward potting compost, John Innes No.1 ensuring the most compact and stable habit of growth and enabling the bulbs to retain sufficient energy to still be a viable proposition when planted out in the garden after flowering is over. Hyacinths and tulips prosper in bulb fibre, but are rarely worth planting into the garden after forcing. Some of the narcissus can be used for naturalizing, but the popular Christmas-flowering paper-white variety is not tough enough to withstand the vigours of open ground cultivation in any but the mildest parts of the country.

Small bulbs, including both tulips and narcissus, should be planted in the pots or bowls in which they are to flower. Hyacinths are best planted in boxes to begin with, unless you are just growing three bulbs in a single bowl, in which case direct planting is necessary (Fig.10). Of all the Christmas-flowering subjects, hyacinths are the most popular, but they are not the easiest bulbs for achieving a visually attractive result. Often the flowers open at different times and the heights appear variable. This is why box culture is advocated at the outset. Provided a single variety is

Lilium candidum, the Madonna lily, is one of the earliest flowering and easiest to grow.

Madonna lilies have long been cultivated in European gardens and are particularly suited to more traditional settings.

Fig. 10 Hyacinths in bowls should be planted with just their noses protruding.

grown it should make progress at an even rate and flower at a given time. Variation within individual plants will ensure that in practice this is not so, but by growing one variety you are going to come as near that ideal as possible. By establishing the bulbs in a box, it is possible, prior to introducing the bulbs to the light and warmth of the living room, to lift those of similar stature and state of growth and to plant them in bowls together. If you take a sharp knife and cut through the matted root growth the bulbs can be easily lifted with a cube of root and will grow on without check.

When the bulbs have been planted, plunge the pots or bowls outside in a generous layer of peat or ashes (Fig.11a–c). Alternatively they can be placed in a cool, dark place in the home – usually either the cupboard under the stairs or the garage are ideal. If you leave them inside, then check regularly for watering. Those outside generally receive enough moisture quite naturally. Leave the bulbs undisturbed for a period of at least ten weeks – fourteen weeks for tulips – before bringing them in. At this stage they should be showing bold yellowish shoots which will quickly turn green when exposed to daylight. Clean the pots up, and in the case

of hyacinths you may like to add a small fern to the centre of the bowl in the same way as the florist does. Those popularly used in the flower trade are *Pteris tremula* and *P. cretica albo-lineata*. These are often sold for bottle gardens as well and can usually be picked up as small plants quite cheaply at the local garden centre.

When forcing bulbs the tendency is to want to apply a lot of heat in order to hurry them along, especially if you are trying to achieve flowering by a given date. This is fatal, for uncontrolled forcing by the application of a high temperature results in the etiolation of stems and leaves, together with the collapse of the blossoms. What is required is a balance of heat and light intensity. Winter light is poor and it takes relatively little warmth to throw plant growth out of natural balance. Ordinary room temperature demands that the emerging bulbs are kept in full light in a west- or south-facing window throughout the daylight period. If the bulbs still start to look drawn, then remove them to a cooler room, at the same time providing them with the maximum daylight possible.

Feeding can also distort growth. It used to be thought that feeding could only be undertaken successfully with indoor bulbs from the time that the buds were showing colour. Certainly considerable benefits have been conferred upon bulbs treated this way, using either a traditional multi-purpose liquid feed or a tomato feed every two or three weeks until the foliage faded away. This helps to rebuild the exhausted bulbs for next season and hopefully make it worthwhile planting them out in the garden for the following year. With the exception of hyacinths this seems to be the case, but hyacinths generally deteriorate so badly after forcing that they are not worth planting out in the garden. If they do flower the following spring the heads are usually distorted, with the individual blossoms far apart on the stems.

Recent experiments have somewhat altered our views on feeding regimes. It has been proved quite conclusively that, apart from hyacinths, much better flower and foliage quality can be obtained by feeding from the time that the bulbs are brought into the light and warmth. Hyacinths respond negatively, produc-

Fig. 11a   Plunge bulbs outside in their pots on a level surface.

Fig. 11b   Cover the pots with sand.

Fig. 11c   Leave the buried bulbs outside in the cool for a minimum of ten weeks. Ensure that the top surface of the sand is below the damp-proof course in the brickwork.

ing large rank leaves and long, twisting, serpentine flower stems. They grow completely out of character and are ruined from the point of view of display. The substitution of potting composts for bulb fibre in all cases except hyacinths also give early indications that where nutrients are readily available, then the plants make better progress. A note of caution though: if you are using a potting compost for your bulbs, go easy on the liquid feed, for over-feeding results in soft unnatural growth that is vulnerable to every disease going.

Once forced bulbs are over they should really be discarded, for even though it is possible to take care of them until the foliage fades away, in practice they are usually neglected once the floral show is over. If you are not prepared to give your bulbs the attention they need after flowering, then do not bother. The gardens of the world are littered with poor weedy bulbs that have been tipped out of dried up compost from bowls and have never made the grade again. Most will come round in a couple of years if pampered, but it is best to separate the outside display from the indoor enterprise

57

Lilium 'Fire King' lights up a traditional border. Bulbs and herbaceous plants mixing harmoniously.

Lilium 'Harmony' is a popular modern garden variety well suited to the garden or pot and other containers.

and plant good bulbs in each, rather than use the garden as a repository for the retired inhabitants of the window sill. If you feel that you must plant exhausted bulbs out, then do not do so until the foliage has faded and the bulbs have become dormant. Even though the popularly-forced varieties of bulbs are hardy, their foliage is very vulnerable to damage when raised in warmth and then taken out into the cold spring air. Damaged foliage will affect the efficiency of the storage system in the bulb, vital if a show of flowers is hoped for next season.

SPRING BULBS

The cultivation of spring-flowering bulbs in pots and bowls is similar to that described for Christmas-flowering subjects. By and large they are the same bulbs, perhaps in different varieties, but with the same habits. You can plant much later if a specific flowering date is not required, but it is not possible to skimp on the time that must elapse between planting and bringing into the house. That is vital. The compost or bulb fibre that is used is the same, and as with all bulb planting enterprises, choose the largest size bulb that you can afford in order to secure the best show possible.

When selecting hyacinths for indoor work, be satisfied with nothing less than 20–22 cm (8–9 in) in circumference. Multinosed narcissus are essential for pot culture and so are top-sized tulips with their tunics intact. Smaller bulbs are difficult to be specific about, but all should look firm, clean and meaty.

The diversity of bulbs that can be grown indoors and forced into flower a little ahead of time is legion. Hyacinths are amongst the best, especially varieties like the lovely red 'Jan Bos', blue 'Ostara', 'Pink Pearl' and snowy-white 'L'Innocence'. Within the *Tazetta* narcissus division, 'Paper White' and 'Soleil d'Or' are well suited to the living room, but more traditional daffodils like 'King Alfred', 'Golden Master' and 'Spellbinder' are equally amenable. So too is the *Poeticus* division like 'Actaea' and 'Pheasant's Eye', the varieties usually referred to by gardeners as narcissus. They have flat white petals with a small frilled edged cup of yellow or red. Tulips are very good for pot culture, especially the single early division. The scarlet 'Brilliant Star', golden-yellow 'Bellona' and red and yellow 'Kreizerskroon' are extremely popular. For really early flowering choose a named variety of *Tulipa kaufmanniana* like the red and white 'Heart's Delight' or red and yellow 'Stresa'. *Tulipa fosteriana* varieties include the dazzling 'Red Emperor' and bright yellow 'Easter Parade'.

Amongst the smaller bulbs the bright blue grape hyacinths *Muscari armeniacum* and fully double 'Blue Spike' are eminently suited to indoor culture provided the temperature is not too high. Snowdrops and crocus are very good too, the bunch flowered *Crocus chrysanthus* cultivars like 'Cream Beauty', 'Snow Bunting' and the blue and white 'Lady Killer' being better than the larger-flowered sorts. These only seem at home in a crocus pot (a much reduced version of the popular strawberry pot) but even then they appear a little ungainly.

Chionodoxa luciliae, glory of the snow, is very good in shallow pans; so too are the many varieties of the early dwarf spring flowering *Iris reticulata*. The ordinary species is largely superseded by named kinds like the pale blue 'Cantab', plum-purple 'J.S. Dijt' and mid-blue 'Harmony'. The white *I. vartani alba* and bright yellow *I. danfordiae* are equally amenable, but like all bulbous iris prefer cool, but frost-free conditions. These and the much earlier flowering *Iris histrioides* 'Major' are perfect for cultivation in a sun lounge or unheated porch.

SUMMER BULBS

Of course spring is not the only time when bulbs can be advanced or protected by pot culture. Many of the summer-flowering lilies enjoy pot cultivation and a number are now sold by florists as pot plants. These are mostly varieties known as Mid-Century Hybrids, a race of brightly coloured characters with bold, exotic blossoms. Usually growing up to a metre (3¼ ft) high, they are often artificially dwarfed by the nursery trade and during their second season will revert to their full height. While it is possible for the home gardener to get growth retardent, it is a hazardous business applying it to small numbers of plants. Even when applied properly some early foliage burning results. Most gardeners grow lilies in pots the natural way, merely protecting their blossoms from adverse weather.

Treat them exactly the same way as you would if cultivating them in the open ground, but plant towards the bottom of the pot. Cover with compost, but do not fill the pot up. As the stem grows, gradually fill the pot with growing medium. Many lilies are stem rooted and this enables them to behave normally and provides additional support. Only the very tall kinds demand staking when growing indoors. When this is the case, strong canes should be introduced at the same time that the bulbs are planted so that they are not disturbed. Apart from support the remaining cultivation is as recommended in the open. Plenty of moisture and a little shade from bright sunshine are desirable, as is the removal of the pollen bearing anthers from white-flowered varieties. The anthers can be removed as soon as pollen appears and this prevents the yellow dust from staining and spoiling the blossoms.

OTHER INDOOR BULBS

Amaryllis

Apart from hardy bulbs that can be manipulated to flower at different periods, there are several other worthwhile subjects that are intended specifically for indoor cultivation. Amongst these the amaryllis are favourites. These are regal flowers of enormous proportions with large trumpet-shaped blossoms in vivid hues which are carried on a stout stem above narrow green leaves. They are easily grown to perfection on the living room window sill.

Gardeners who are used to planting more usual bulbs, like daffodils and narcissus, will be amazed by the size of the amaryllis bulb. Even modest ones are as big as a grapefruit. The startling blossom is already present in the dormant bulb in embryo form. So the bigger the bulb, the larger the blossom. Surprisingly amaryllis do not require an enormous pot in order to flourish. Unlike most other bulbs, they benefit from being tightly potted. Use a John Innes No.3 potting compost, and when potting allow just enough room to pack the compost down the side with your fingers. Stand the pot in a light sunny window and water regularly, using a liquid house-plant feed once flower buds are seen. Bring the pot back into the room during the evening, for amaryllis are not happy with the cool conditions behind closed curtains.

After flowering, the old flower stem should be removed as close to the bulb as possible, but feeding should be continued until the middle of summer. Regular feeding, combined with healthy foliage will build up the bulb for next year. Aim to have at least four good strong leaves all the time and next year's blossom will then be assured. Although in their native home amaryllis grow all the year round, a short resting period is very beneficial. In early autumn withhold watering and place the pot on its side in a cool well ventilated place until the foliage has died back completely. Restart into growth during early spring using fresh compost and providing a warm environment. Given this treatment your amaryllis can become an annual delight. Most gardeners begin by growing unnamed bulbs, but with experience will often seek some of the very fine-named varieties. There are some lovely sorts like the pale pink 'Apple Blossom', red and white 'Minerva' as well as the vivid 'Orange Sovereign'.

Sprekelia

There is also an interesting relative of the amaryllis called *Sprekelia formosissima*. Becoming increasingly popular, this is a much hardier character with striking solitary red flowers of deep scarlet. These can be pro-

Crinum powellii is a majestic autumn flowering bulb for a sheltered spot at the base of a wall.

Mixed crocus make an early spring spectacle scattered amongst still sleeping shrubs. Most multiply freely if left undisturbed.

duced at any time from spring until mid-summer amongst narrow linear leaves. Often sold by nurseries as the Jacobean lily, sprekelia is best potted in John Innes No.3 potting compost during late summer or early autumn, established clumps being periodically divided at that time too. Provided it is given a sunny spot on the window sill and not allowed to go short of water, it should prosper.

Begonia

Similar conditions suit begonias. Tuberous begonias with their flouncing blossoms are the queens of the summer display. They are richly coloured exotic plants that are amongst the easiest to grow. There are fully double varieties, frilled and carnation-flowered sorts as well as the graceful, pendant kinds. All are easy to grow and have a long flowering period.

The coarse brown tubers should be purchased in early spring, but it depends upon the kind of conditions which you have as to whether you plant them during early spring, or leave them until later. If you can provide a temperature of 16–18 °C (61–64 °F), then get them planted early. Otherwise leave them until the end of mid-spring. Gardeners are often mystified as to how to plant the tubers. One side is coarse and concave while the other is rounded and smooth. Always ensure that the rough concave side is upwards, for it is from here that the roots and shoots develop. If you only have one or two tubers they can be planted individually in pots, but if you have many they are best started in boxes. A compost of equal parts, John Innes potting compost No.2 and moss peat, provide the ideal growing medium, the tubers being planted so that they are scarcely covered. Keep well watered and cover with brown paper to protect the emerging roots from bright sunlight, only removing the paper when small shoots are seen.

When leaves start to appear the tubers will have developed a good root system and can then be potted individually. For a really good show of high quality blossoms it is vital to remove all but the strongest

shoot, unless grown in a hanging container. If this is done when the shoots are 5–8 cm (2–3 in) long, then they can be rooted as cuttings and will quickly become new plants. Once well established, after three weeks or so, introduce a potash feed to aid stable development. Never use a fertilizer that is high in nitrogen as this promotes soft sappy growth that is vulnerable to both rots and mildew. The really large double-flowered begonias benefit from staking, slim green canes and raffia or twist ties being adequate. In order to produce large individual flowers all the buds in the cluster can be reduced to the strongest individual. In fully double flowered varieties the female flowers should be removed as these are single, insignificant, and a drain upon the plant's resources, for they are only intent upon producing seed. It is the little winged seed capsule behind every female flower that gives it away, even in the bud stage.

Begonias are easy-going and require little attention throughout the summer months. Ensure that they are well watered and remove blossoms as they fade. For very little effort you can have a glorious show of colour from mid-summer until the autumn. However, they benefit from a rest, and as autumn progresses they should be gradually dried off prior to storing. Turn the pots on their side and allow the foliage to die back naturally. Then cut it away and remove the tubers, dusting with flowers of sulphur to help prevent fungal infections and storage moulds, and place in a box of dry peat. Store at a temperture of 5–7 °C (41–45 °F) periodically checking the tubers for any signs of decay. The following spring the tubers can be potted once again and you can look forward to another colour-filled summer.

Gloriosa

Adventurous gardeners should try growing the gloriosa lilies. Until the past few years these have been looked upon as being tropical and rather exotic, a little beyond the gardener without a greenhouse. Recent experience has shown that it is possible to accommodate at least two species in the living room. Natives of tropical Asia, it is *Gloriosa rothschildiana* and *G. superba* that are being widely popularized. Each has handsome glossy green foliage on strong wiry stems which yield showy red and yellow or orange-red blossoms.

Unlike true lilies, the bulbous roots of gloriosa do not consist of myriad scales but are smooth, whitish, elongated rootstocks, rather finger-like in appearance. Plant them horizontally 4–5 cm (1½–2 in) below the surface of the compost. Put several in a large pot and use a peaty compost with a generous quantity of grit added to assist with drainage. A mixture based upon a soil-less potting compost is ideal. There is always conflicting advice when gloriosas should be planted. If you can provide no heat or frost protection then leave it until mid-summer. Immediately after planting prepare a support for the plants as they scramble around freely once started into growth. A framework with slender wires suits them best, rather than a robust wooden trellis. Once the plants are growing strongly they must be fed at fortnightly intervals with a liquid house-plant feed, but this should be withdrawn as autumn approaches. As the plants die down naturally watering should cease and the roots allowed to dry out. The rootstocks can be lifted and stored in a frost-free place in a tray of peat for the winter months. Alternatively the pots can be turned on their sides and the roots kept dry. The following spring or early summer they should be removed and planted in fresh compost.

Zantedeschia

Apart from the bulbs that can be grown successfully in the house, there are several that really need a greenhouse to do them justice. Amongst these one of the loveliest groups comprises the arum lilies. The white arum lily, *Zantedeschia aethiopica* is one of the finest decorative greenhouse subjects. With pure white spathes amidst glossy dark green foliage, it provides endless pleasure throughout late spring and early summer. The ordinary species is the best loved, but if you have limited space, then either 'Little Gem' or 'God-frey', neither of which grow more than 45 cm (1½ ft) high, are an acceptable alternative.

Semi-dormant tubers can be planted in large pots during late summer or early autumn in John Innes potting compost No.3. If ample warmth can be provided, then growth will be steady, the first flower buds appearing during early spring. When these are forming, an ordinary house-plant feed is beneficial and this should be continued until flowering is over. Once the spathes have faded the plants can be stood outside in a cold frame for the summer months. Although they should not be allowed to dry out completely, the tubers should be encouraged to rest, prior to being repotted again during late summer or early autumn. At this time keep an eye open for tiny suckers which cluster around the main tuber. These can be removed and potted individually to form new plants.

Apart from the more familiar white species there are a number of other arums of similar habit and appearance: *Zantedeschia elliotiana* is the most handsome, sporting deep yellow spathes amongst dark green leaves that are liberally splashed and blotched with silver and white. *Z. rehmanii* is popularly referred to as the pink arum, while 'Helen O'Conner' is a bold apricot colour. Apart from being raised from detached suckers this can also be grown easily from seed. All require similar conditions to the white arum, but appreciate a higher temperature, 20–25 °C (68–77 °F) not being excessive.

The voodoo lily, *Sauromatum guttatum* is often classified as an arum and popularly sold as a bulb for indoor or greenhouse decoration. Botanically a member of the arum lily family it has a large upright purplish green spathe spotted with purple. Also known as monarch of the east, it is the variety *venosum* with its paler, more yellowish spathes heavily splashed and spotted with crimson that is most likely to be seen at the garden centre. The flowers are produced at most seasons of the year, depending upon when you buy the dry bulb, but always appear before the dull green foliage. It is usually stood in a saucer on the window ledge and allowed to flower from the dry bulb, but can be treated in the same manner as an arum lily.

Colourful crocus announce the awakening of the garden from its winter slumber. Scatter them freely amongst shrubs and border plants.

SELECTED SPRING-FLOWERING BULBS FOR GROWING INDOORS

There are many different varieties of bulbs for forcing and bringing into flower early. Some of the best are listed here. All require a cool dark period of between 10 and 14 weeks before being brought into the warmth. The minimum periods are noted against each variety in weeks.

Bulb	Weeks
Hyacinths	
Specially prepared	11
Ordinary bulbs	12
'Amsterdam' (red)	12
'Bismarck' (blue)	12
'L'Innocence' (white)	12
'Jan Bos' (red)	12
'Pink Pearl' (pink)	12
Tulips	
'Brilliant Star' (red)	10
'Christmas Marvel' (carmine)	10
'Joffre' (yellow)	10
'Apricot Beauty' (apricot)	10
'Kees Nelis' (red, edged yellow)	10
'Mirjoran' (red, edged cream)	10
'Merry Widow' (red, edged white)	16
'Monte Carlo' (yellow)	14
'Paul Richter' (red)	14
'Prominence' (dark red)	14
'Stockholm' (scarlet)	14
'Charles' (scarlet, yellow base)	14

Bulb	Weeks
Daffodils	
'Barrett Browning' (white & flame)	14
'Carlton' (uniform yellow)	14
Cyclamineus 'February Gold' (yellow)	14
'Jenny' (white)	14
'Peeping Tom' (yellow)	14
'Dutch Master' (soft yellow)	14
'Flower Record' (white & yellow)	14
'Fortune' (yellow & orange)	14
'Golden Harvest' (golden yellow)	14
'Ice Follies' (white)	14
'Peeping Tom' (yellow)	14
'Professor Einstein' (white & orange)	14
'Verger' (white & deep red)	14
'Yellow Sun' (clear yellow	14
Crocus Dutch varieties	14
Crocus chrysanthus and varieties	16
Snowdrop single and double	14
Iris danfordiae	12
I. histrioides	12
I.h. 'Major'	12
Iris reticulata varieties	14
Muscari armeniacum	16
Puschkinia libanotica	16
Scilla sibirica	16
S. tubergeniana	16

7

BULB PROBLEMS

As bulbs push through the soil, keep an eye open for any signs of distress caused by the various pests and diseases which trouble these colourful subjects. Bulbs that have been purchased from a reliable source can usually be counted upon to be free from all fungal diseases for the first season, but they will nevertheless be just as vulnerable to attacks by slugs, snails and other pests as their established counterparts. Slugs and snails can be controlled by regular applications of slug bait scattered amongst the plants. A ring of coarse ash, sand or similar abrasive material placed around groups of bulbs will also act as a deterrent.

Leatherjackets and wireworms are not so easily dealt with, for they live exclusively beneath the soil, feeding on the bulbs and causing their eventual collapse. An insecticidal dust worked around the bulbs during early spring, when the grubs are near the surface of the soil, should in most situations help to bring about a reasonable control.

Narcissus, hyacinths and scillas are often attacked by the larvae of the narcissus fly. This is a voracious feeder which burrows into bulbs causing them to become soft, spongy and eventually rot away. The leaves, even if they appear, are weak and twisted and inspection of a lifted bulb will reveal a fat white grub nestling amongst festering brown leaf scales. Any bulbs found in this condition must be burnt, and plants of other closely related species that still appear to be healthy should be dusted with lindane during late spring and early summer when the adult flies are busy laying their eggs.

Stem and bulb eelworms attack almost all the popular spring bulbs. These are minute nematode worms, invisible to the naked eye, which invade all living tissues of the plants and cause gross malformation. Leaves become twisted, flowers distorted, and brown rings or patches appear on the bulb scales. There is no easy cure and infected bulbs should be destroyed and the ground on which they were growing kept free from bulbs for three of four years.

Although not so numerous, the various types of bulb diseases can be equally devastating. Most come under the general heading of botrytis, and although they manifest themselves in many different ways, all can be controlled with a considerable degree of success by spraying with Bordeaux mixture at the first sign. One of the most common botrytis diseases attacks narcissus and hyacinths. This is known as smoulder and causes the leaves to turn yellow and wilt. Snowdrops, on the other hand, sometimes suffer from a disease called grey mould which invades the leaves and bulbs causing extensive rotting and the entire collapse of the plant.

From the foregoing you might be surprised to see any healthy bulbs at all, but all is not gloom and despondency, for careful cultivation, coupled with the selection of healthy stock in the first place, will give every chance of a trouble-free display.

PROBLEM-FINDER CHART

BULBS, CORMS AND TUBERS
BEFORE PLANTING

Symptoms	Cause	Treatment
Soft and slimy	Bacterial Soft Rot	Burn diseased material and do not plant fresh stock in the same soil for several years.
Decomposing and covered in blue-green mould	Blue Mould Rot	Always handle bulbs carefully to restrict damage and place of entry for the disease. Dip in a suspension of benomyl for 15–30 minutes before planting.
Surface damage and evidence of shiny white, hairy, mites	Bulb Mite	Discard and burn infested bulbs.
Soft, with decaying centre. Maggots often present. Narcissus and hyacinth particularly vulnerable	Narcissus Fly	Heat-treated bulbs are free from this pest. Dust around growing bulbs with H.C.H. dust during summer when flies are on the wing. Burn infected material.
Soft, with circles of brown discoloured tissue internally	Stem Eelworm	Destroy affected bulbs and do not replant in the same area for at least three years.

AFTER PLANTING

Symptoms	Cause	Treatment
Plants produce leaves, but fail to flower	Blindness	Exposing bulbs to high temperatures after lifting sometimes cures the problem.
Bulbs, leaves and stems chewed off at ground level or beneath soil. Grubs seen	Cutworms	Expose infested soil to winter weather and dust liberally with H.C.H. dust before planting and around existing bulbs.

Chart continued on page 72

Dutch crocus or 'fat boys' defy harsh winter weather to push forth colourful golden chalices.

The icy-white blossoms of the common snowdrop are highlighted by the dark backdrop of the ivy, 'Paddy's Pride'.

PROBLEM-FINDER CHART – *continued from page 69*

Symptoms	Cause	Treatment
Leaves thin and grassy, flowers weak and twisted	Narcissus Fly	Heat-treated bulbs are free from this pest. Dust around growing bulbs with H.C.H. dust during summer when flies are on the wing. Burn infected material.
Irregular holes in parts of the plant below and at soil level	Slugs	Scatter slug pellets around plants especially in early spring. Maintain good garden hygiene and improve drainage where possible.
Leaves poor, twisted and discoloured, occasionally displaying yellow bumps or patches	Stem Eelworm	Destroy affected bulbs and do not replant in the same area for at least three years.
Roots eaten away, small white grubs present, especially indoors	Vine Weevil	Dust soil with H.C.H. and for pot- and container-grown bulbs mix in with the compost at planting time.
Base of plant and bulb rots leaving matted dark strands	Violet Root Rot	Burn infected plants and attempt to improve drainage.
Neat holes in fleshy underground stems and storage organs, occasionally small buff or orange-yellow wiry grubs present	Wireworms	Dust soil with H.C.H. before planting and occasionally around the plants during the summer months.

APPENDIX 1

SELECTING AND BUYING BULBS

Purchase and plant bulbs as early in the season as possible. The sooner that they get into the ground the less likely they are to suffer from dehydration. Bulbs lying in polythene bags on a supermarket shelf in warm conditions deteriorate rapidly. Choose your bulbs from a supplier who is able to keep them cool and dry. Whenever possible select your own bulbs, discarding anything that is soft or obviously discoloured. With narcissus (Fig.12), feel the base plate where the roots sprout from and if it feels soft pass it over. Avoid crocus (Fig.13), gladioli and tulips that have lost their tunics. The skins of bulbs provide protection, and when planted without it they are vulnerable to all kinds of diseases and disorders. Snowdrops should be carefully inspected for signs of grey mould and the tiny bulbous iris must have clean white or cream skins. If you see black spots on the tunics avoid them as they are likely to be suffering from the debilitating and very contagious ink spot disease. Large bulbs of any variety always yield the best results, so go for the biggest that you can afford. Multi-nosed narcissus are also an excellent buy.

Fig. 13   Structure of a crocus corm.

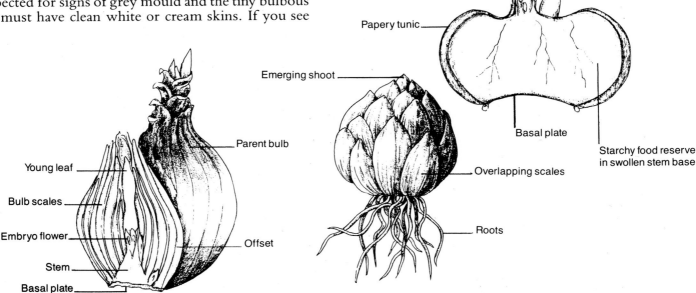

Fig. 13 labels: New leaf, Embryo flower, Papery tunic, Shoot, Basal plate, Starchy food reserve in swollen stem base

Fig. 12 labels: Young leaf, Bulb scales, Embryo flower, Stem, Basal plate, Parent bulb, Offset

Fig. 14 labels: Emerging shoot, Overlapping scales, Roots

Fig. 12   Structure of a daffodil bulb.

Fig. 14   A lily bulb is composed almost entirely of leaf scales.

Nerine bowdenii flowers during the autumn. It must have a well-drained soil in a sunny position, preferably at the base of a wall.

APPENDIX 2

PROPAGATING BULBS AND CORMS

Many bulbs produce bulbils around mature adult bulbs. These need lifting every three or four years and the young bulbs removed and planted separately. If left to become a congested mass they deteriorate. It is important to check when you remove any young bulb from the adult that it has an independent base plate from which roots can grow. Bulbils torn away from the parent have little chance of survival and leave the mature bulb open to infection. Selected youngsters can be lined out in a nursery bed until of flowering size and ready for planting out in their permanent positions. With bulbs like tulips, that are lifted regularly after a bedding display, the daughter bulbs will be evident and can be removed when sufficiently well developed. These also need planting out in a nursery bed initially.

Corms, like gladioli and crocus, replace themselves annually, tiny cormlets or spawn (Fig.15) clustering around the adults. Gather the cormlets and plant them in a seed tray of soil-based potting compost. When they are large enough to withstand the rough and tumble of the garden, get them planted out. Some of the smaller bulbs, like grape hyacinths, behave in a similar manner. Separate out the young bulbils and plant immediately as they do not have a very good protective skin and rapidly dry out when exposed to the air.

Hyacinths occasionally produce one or two young bulbils around the base plate, but this is largely a matter of chance. To ensure a good crop of fry it is essential to damage the base plate. Take a mature healthy bulb and turn it upside down, slashing the conspicuous circular base plate with a sharp knife. Remove two slivers of tissue to form a cross. It is along the line of this incision that the bulbils will cluster. Be careful not to damage the soft tissue of the bulb when making the incision as this leaves an entry for fungal diseases. Plant the slashed bulb in a large pot or box of good friable compost and grow on as normal. Masses of bulbils will congregate along the incisions and these can be removed when the bulb dies back naturally. Planted individually in trays of a soil-based compost they should grow away quickly, the young bulbs eventually being removed to a nursery bed outside. Flowering size takes about four years to develop.

Some bulbs can be raised from seed. This is predominantly the smaller growing species. Seed gathered from a named variety is likely to be of hybrid

Fig. 15 A freshly lifted gladiolus showing both old and new corms and spawn.

origin and mostly inferior to its parents. Raising bulbs from seed is a long job, even the quickest subjects taking three or more years to flower, but it is often the only way of obtaining stock of the unusual. The seed of bulbous subjects should be sown in pans of John Innes seed compost and placed in a frame. Some kinds germinate rapidly, while others require freezing in order to break dormancy. All look like grasses when they first emerge and they should be allowed to become well established before being pricked out.

APPENDIX 3

CUT FLOWER BULBS

Even if you do not grow bulbs specifically for cut flowers, the temptation to cut a few blossoms for the house is irresistible. With proper care most of the popular kinds, like tulips, gladioli and Dutch iris, can have a long vase life. After picking and taking them into the house, always cut off the bottom part of the stem under water to prevent air being trapped in the stem and restricting water uptake. If you are using sensitive flowers like tulips it is a good idea to wrap the flowers in paper and stand them in cold water initially. This helps prevent them from hanging their heads when first taken into the living room. Of course it is important that the paper does not touch the water. If the flowers flag after a couple of days the treatment can be repeated. Remember also that most flowers continue to grow when put in water, so ensure that the vase is sufficiently deep to prevent them from becoming twisted. Always use fresh water, preferably incorporating cut flower nutrition, and place the vase in a cool place overnight.

Most bulb flowers mix amicably with one another and with flowers from shrubby or herbaceous plants. However, recent research has shown that the addition of daffodils to mixed arrangements causes their rapid deterioration unless suitable action is taken. The problem arises from the water-soluble slime which daffodils produce from their cut stems. This is toxic to other cut flowers, especially roses, tulips, freesias, anemones and carnations. If you wish to mix daffodils with other cut flowers, stand them on their own in water for 24 hours and then wash the stems. There should then be no problem unless you decide to cut the end of the stems when the flowers are being arranged. As a further precaution add activated charcoal to the vase water to absorb the slime. Being powdered this does not mix very well with the water, so put the charcoal in first and then add the water, stirring steadily all the time - 1 tablespoon of activated charcoal to 1 litre (1¾ pints) of water.

Alternatively household chlorine can be added to the water (5–7 drops of concentrate to 1 litre (1¾ pints) of water). This has a beneficial effect as long as the ratio of daffodils to other flowers is approximately equal. When daffodils outnumber other flowers, then more chlorine needs to be added and this may cause damage to more sensitive subjects.

APPENDIX 4: CLASSIFICATION

Table 1. Divisions of Daffodils and Narcissus

The term trumpet or cup is here embraced by the term corona. The perianth segments are what the gardener would call petals.

Division 1: TRUMPET DAFFODIL VARIETIES
One flower to a stem; trumpet or corona as long, or longer than the perianth segments.

Division 2: LONG-CUPPED DAFFODIL VARIETIES
One flower to a stem; cup or corona more than one-third, but less than equal to the length of the perianth segments.

Division 3: SHORT-CUPPED DAFFODIL VARIETIES
One flower to a stem; cup or corona not more than one-third the length of the perianth segments.

Division 4: DOUBLE DAFFODIL VARIETIES
Double flowers.

Division 5: TRIANDRUS DAFFODIL VARIETIES
Characteristics of *Narcissus triandrus* predominant.

Division 6: CYCLAMINEUS DAFFODIL VARIETIES
Characteristics of *Narcissus cyclamineus* predominant.

Division 7: JONQUILLA DAFFODIL VARIETIES
Characteristics of *Narcissus jonquilla* predominant.

Division 8: TAZETTA DAFFODIL VARIETIES
Characteristics of *Narcissus tazetta* predominant.

Division 9: POETICUS DAFFODIL VARIETIES
Characteristics of *Narcissus poeticus* predominant.

Division 10: SPECIES, WILD FORMS AND WILD HYBRIDS
All species and wild, or reputedly wild, forms and hybrids. Double forms of these varieties are included.

Division 11: SPLIT – CORONA DAFFODIL VARIETIES
Corona split for at least 1/3 of its length.

Division 12: MISCELLANEOUS DAFFODILS
All daffodils not falling into any one of the foregoing Divisions.

Table 2. Classification of Garden Tulips

SINGLE EARLY
This is one of the earliest flowering tulip groups. They generally are 25-35 cm (10–14 in) tall.

DOUBLE EARLY
These early tulips have double flowers which resemble paeonies. Average plant height is 25-30 cm (10–12 in).

TRIUMPH
These were developed from a cross between single early and late-flowering varieties. This group produces angular flowers and lance-shaped leaves that sometimes have a glaucous tinge. Average height: 30–35 cm.

DARWIN HYBRIDS
These are the result of crossing Darwin tulips with *T. fosteriana*. They have great vigour and are excellent for bedding. All have a characteristic satiny sheen to the petals and a large flower size. Average plant height: 35–45 cm (14–18)in.

SINGLE LATE TULIPS
This class includes Darwin Tulips and Cottage Tulips. Owing to hybridization, the borderlines between the former classes are no longer discernible.

Chart continued on page 78

LILY-FLOWERED
These produce flowers with petals that are pointed and turned outwards at the tips. Lance-shaped leaves. Average plant height is 40–45 cm (16–18 in).

FRINGED TULIPS
Tulips with petals that are edged with crystal-shaped fringes.

VIRIDIFLORA TULIPS
Tulips with partly greenish petals.

REMBRANDT
These tulips are similar to Darwin varieties except the flower colouring is broken.

PARROT
These produce lance-shaped leaves, sometimes with a glaucous tinge. The often bicoloured flowers have twisted and irregularly fringed petals. Flowers open in mid- to late-spring and measure 20 cm (8 in) or more across. Average plant height is 40–45 cm (16–18 in).

DOUBLE LATE TULIPS
This group has long-lasting flowers which resemble paeonies and have lance-shaped leaves. Average plant height is 36 cm (14 in).

T.kaufmanniana
Tulips known as waterlily tulips. Produce glaucous-green leaves. Average plant height is 22 cm (9 in).

T.fosteriana
Tulips with large flowers and grey-green leaves. Average plant height is 30 cm (12 in).

T. greigii
Tulips producing outstanding broad glaucous-green leaves which are heavily mottled with brown or purple. The petals are reflexed at the tips. Average plant height is 30 cm (12 in).

Other Species
Miscellaneous grouping of all other species and their hybrids.

INDEX

Acidanthera, 28
Aconite, winter, 7, 36–37
Aftercare of bulbs, 13–16
Allium, 7, 12
   giganteum, 13
   moly, 13
   ostrowskianum, 13
   sphaerocephalum, 13
Alpine bulbs, 16–17
   meadows, 18–20
Amaryllis belladonna, 36, 61
Anemone blanda, 7, 49
   De Caen, 32, 52
   St Brigid, 32, 52
Autumn bulbs, 33–40

Bedding with bulbs, 44–47
Begonia, 64
Blue mould rot, 69
Bluebell, 20
Botritis, 68
Bulb mite, 69
Buying bulbs, 7–8, 73

Canna, 49, 52
Chincherinchee, 29, 32
Chionodoxa luciliae, 9, 49, 52, 53, 60
Christmas flowering bulbs, 53–60
Colchicum, 52
   speciosum, 33
Composts, 48
Crinum powellii, 36
Crocosmia crocosmiiflora, 29
Crocus, 37, 49, 52, 67
   autumn, 33
   chrysanthus, 37, 49, 60, 67
   propagation, 75
   sativus, 33
   speciosus, 33
Crown imperial, 7, 12
Cut flowers from bulbs, 76
Cutworms, 69

Cyclamen, 52
   neapolitanum, 52
   repandum, 52

Daffodils *see Narcissus*
Diseases, 68–72
Drainage, 49

Eelworms, 68, 69, 72
Endymion campanulatus, 20
   hispanicus, 20
Eranthis hyemalis, 36–37, 52
Eremurus, 7
Erythronium dens-canis, 52
Eucomis bicolor, 29

Feeding, 56
Forcing, 53–60
Formal planting, 41–44
Fritillaria camschatcensis, 12
   imperialis, 7, 12
   meleagris, 12, 18
   persica, 12
   pyreniaca, 12

Galanthus corycensis, 37
   elwesii, 52
   nivalis, 17, 37, 52
Galtonia candicans, 29
   princeps, 29
Gladiolus, 25–28, 75
   nanus, 26
Gloriosa, 64
   rothschildiana, 65
   superba, 65
Glory of the snow, 9, 49
Grey mould, 68
Guinea flower, 12

Harlequin flower, 28–29
Hyacinth, 45–46, 52, 53, 56–57, 60, 67
   grape, 7, 49

propagation, 75
   summer, 29

Indoor bulbs, 53–67
Iris, 13
   bakeriana, 17
   danfordiae, 17, 40, 52, 60, 67
   histrio, 17
   histrioides, 17, 60, 67
   reticulata, 17, 40, 52, 60, 67
   vartani alba, 40, 60
   winogradowii, 17
Ixia, 29

Leatherjackets, 68
Leucojum aestivum, 37
   vernuum, 37
Light conditions, 56
Lilium, 21–25
   auratum, 24
   candidum, 24
   henryi, 24
   martagon, 24
   Mid-century hybrids, 52, 60–61
   regale, 24
   speciosum, 24
   tigrinum, 24
Lily *see Lilium*
   corn, 29
   foxtail, 7
   Jacobean, 64
   snakeshead, 12, 18

Meadow saffron, 33
Montbretia laxiflora, 29
Muscari, 7
   armeniacum, 9, 49, 52, 60, 67
   botryoides, 12, 52

Naked ladies, 33
Narcissus, 7–8, 41, 47, 53, 67
   asturiensis, 16

INDEX

bulbocodium, 16
canaliculatus, 16
classification, 77
cut flowers, 76
cyclamineus, 7, 16, 17, 47, 49, 52, 67
elegans, 17
hoop petticoat, 18
jonquilla, 52
lobularis, 16, 17
nanus, 16
poeticus, 60
serotinus, 17
tazetta, 60
triandrus albus, 52
viridiflorus, 17
Narcissus fly, 68, 69, 72
Naturalized bulbs, 17–18
Nerine bowdenii, 33, 36

Ornithogalum arabicum, 32
thyrsoides, 29, 32

Pests, 68–72
Pineapple flower, 29

Propagation of bulbs and corms 75–76
Pushkinia libanotica, 52, 67
scilloides, 40

Ranunculus, 32

Scilla non-scripta, 20
sibirica, 7, 30, 49, 52, 67
tubergeniana, 7, 37, 49, 52, 67
Slugs, 68, 72
Smoulder, 68
Snails, 68
Snowdrop, 7, 17, 36–37, 53, 67
Snowflake, 37
Soft rot, 69
Sparaxis, 28–29
Sprekelia formosissima, 61, 64
Spring bulbs, 7–20
for pots, 60
for windowboxes, 49
Squill *see Pushkinia; Scilla*
Sternbergia lutea, 33
Summer bulbs, 21–32
for pots, 60–61
for windowboxes, 49–52

Tigridia, 26
Tulipa, 8–9, 44, 52, 53, 67
classification, 77–78
cut flowers, 76
Darwin, 47
eichleri, 9, 49, 52
fosteriana, 9, 49, 52, 60
greigii, 9, 49, 52
kaufmanniana, 9, 16, 20, 49, 52, 60
linifolia, 16
maximowiczii, 16
praestans, 9, 47, 49, 52
propagation, 75
saxatilis, 9
tarda, 9, 16

Vine weevil, 72
Violet root rot, 72

Wireworms, 68, 72

Zantedeschia aethiopica, 65
elliotiana, 65
rehmanii, 65